**FIFA OFFICIAL LICENSED PUBLICATION**

# THE FOOTBALL PUZZLE BOOK

D1609938

Published in 2021 by Welbeck
an imprint of Welbeck Non-Fiction Limited
part of Welbeck Publishing Group
20 Mortimer Street London W1T 3JW

A CIP catalogue record for this book is available from the British Library

ISBN 978-1-78739-600-5

Printed in Dubai

10 9 8 7 6 5 4 3 2 1

FIFA OFFICIAL LICENSED PUBLICATION

# THE FOOTBALL PUZZLE BOOK

## TACKLE MORE THAN **100** PUZZLES INSPIRED BY THE WORLD'S MOST BEAUTIFUL GAME

DR GARETH MOORE

WELBECK

# CONTENTS

# INTRODUCTION

**Welcome!**

**You've been chosen to represent your country in the beautiful game's most important competition: the FIFA World Cup™. As team captain, you'll be heavily involved in all aspects of decision-making – both in tactical and in training – and you'll need to lead your team from the front in your matches.**

Over the course of this book, you'll complete tasks, activities and challenges and, if you're successful, you'll take your team from the qualifying rounds all the way through to the FIFA World Cup final, before hopefully going on to win it!

The book follows the structure of the FIFA World Cup, with six chapters corresponding in turn to:

- ⚽ **QUALIFYING ROUNDS**
- ⚽ **GROUP STAGE**
- ⚽ **ROUND OF 16**
- ⚽ **QUARTER-FINALS**
- ⚽ **SEMI-FINALS**
- ⚽ **FINAL**

You'll play three games in each of the first two chapters, and then one in each of the remaining chapters – but, along the way, you'll have many other football-related puzzles to overcome. And, just like in the real competition, the challenge you face will increase in difficulty as you advance through the stages. This means that, whenever you encounter an exercise you've already tackled earlier in the competition, you'll find that you need even better tactics than the previous time to succeed, or that some of the goalposts – literally or otherwise – have been moved. Remember never to take your eye off the ball!

There are four types of puzzle page: TRAINING, TACTICS, GAME TIME and VISUAL. The first three of these are explained at the beginning of the qualifying rounds (see page 8), while the VISUAL puzzles spread throughout the competition are, perhaps unsurprisingly, designed to test your observation skills. In the other puzzle types, you'll be drawing lines, shading areas, and placing players and symbols on the field, which is often divided into grid squares.

Besides the book, you'll need very little to complete each task: a sharp pencil and mind, and sometimes a way of timing yourself – a referee's stopwatch would be useful!

## THE REF'S WATCHING!

To help you sharpen your mind and make sure you're in top form to take on the greatest football teams on the international stage, you'll sometimes earn yellow or red cards for mistakes you make – even when in training.

When you complete each puzzle, check your solution against the one given at the back of the book. If you've made a mistake, look at the title of the puzzle in question and note its **first letter**, then take the **last digit** of the puzzle's page number (if it's on multiple pages, use the page number where the title is), and then look these up in the **Referee's Table** on pages 222-223. These codes will also be listed next to the solution. You'll either be shown a yellow or red card. Mark it in the box on page 222.

When you reach a GAME TIME page, work out how many red cards you have (just as in normal football, every two yellow cards become one red card, and any leftover yellow card is ignored). If you have more red cards than the maximum stipulated at the top of the GAME TIME page, then the opposition have scored a penalty. Mark one in the grid on page 223, and remove that number of red and yellow cards from your tally.

For example, if you have earned one red card and three yellow cards, and the GAME TIME puzzle has a maximum of two reds, the opposition have scored a penalty and you can remove the red card and two of the yellow cards from your tally, leaving one yellow card still in your possession.

Fortunately, you have the opportunity to "score" your own penalties by beating certain time limits in training. These chances will be signalled throughout with prompts such as "can you complete the puzzle in two minutes or less to score a penalty?" If you complete those exercises in time, mark your scored penalties in the grid as well. However, take too long and you might get booked, in which case, turn to the ref's grid for a card – just as if you had got the puzzle wrong.

Do you have the skills not only to lift the trophy, but also to beat the book in a penalty shoot-out?

### Good luck!

# QUALIFYING ROUNDS

## Welcome to the FIFA World Cup™!

You've been selected as the team captain – congratulations. There's a lot of responsibility involved, but your manager thinks you have what it takes to lead the squad through the competition. All good managers have a plan and yours is no exception: they've devised a training programme for you and the team to follow, which will cover all aspects of the game and prepare you for the challenges of international football that lie ahead.

**Your time between now and the final – if you get there – will be spent concentrating on three main elements of the game: TRAINING, TACTICS and GAME TIME.**

- In **TRAINING**, you'll focus on fitness exercises and path-finding tests to help you make the most of the on-field playing space.
- **TACTICS** sessions will involve more mental work, and your manager will guide you through exercises designed to help you visualise game play and ensure your team are always in the best position on the pitch.
- When it's finally **GAME TIME**, you'll put your skills to the test in a variety of scenarios, where you'll need to make quick and accurate decisions based on the situation on the pitch in front of you.

Over the next three games, you'll be competing with other teams to earn a place in the competition. After that, it's the group stage – but only if you win your qualifiers first! The finals are a long way off, but there's no time like the present to train and talk tactics.

# WARM-UP

**In your first qualifying match, you're expecting an easy win, but that doesn't mean you can relax – you'll need to put your best feet forward and train as normal so that victory is assured.**

This training exercise is a familiar one. Can you dribble the ball all the way across the pitch, from the goal on the left to the goal on the right, without crossing any of the blue lines? There's only one correct way to do it, and you'll need to keep an eye on the path ahead to make sure you don't get stuck in any dead ends. Your path can't cross itself, either, so make sure you don't get into any corners you can't get out of.

As it's your first training session, the boss wants to test your fitness – in this case, speed is the priority, so set a timer. When you've finished the exercise, check your time against the scoreboard below.

⏱ **How fast can you find your way across the pitch?**

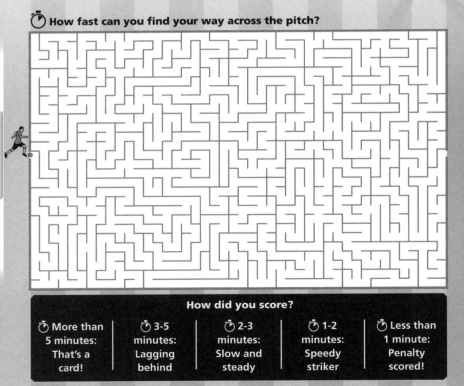

## How did you score?

| ⏱ More than 5 minutes: That's a card! | ⏱ 3-5 minutes: Lagging behind | ⏱ 2-3 minutes: Slow and steady | ⏱ 1-2 minutes: Speedy striker | ⏱ Less than 1 minute: Penalty scored! |

# BALANCING BIBS

**You're through the first physical training session, and now it's time for tactics. Your manager has gathered the whole squad on the pitch, so that everyone has a chance to shine. The first-choice line-up is still not set in stone – as captain, though, you're a pretty safe bet!**

Bibs are handed out to all of the players. Some have an X on and some have an O. But don't worry, this isn't a selection process – it's a test of the team's reactions. The manager asks some of the players to spread out around the pitch, in the formation shown below. The challenge for the remaining players is to fill all of the empty spaces on the pitch so that no four players in a row have the same bib on, including diagonally.

For the exercise to work, the players will have to consider the whole pitch, and expand their focus outside of their immediate field of vision to make sure that no areas become accidentally unbalanced. Can you work out where each player should go, and whether each space should be filled with an X or an O? There may not be the same number of bibs with each symbol.

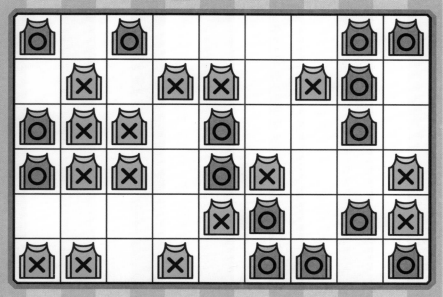

SOLUTION ON PAGE **180**

# TRAINING CONES

**Now that you've had a mental workout from the tactics session, it's time for a jog.**

This time, as well as showing off your speed, you'll be tested on how well you deal with obstacles that block your path. You'll need to prove that you can think ahead and keep the future consequences of your chosen route in mind as you make your way around the pitch. Instead of an opposition team, however, the training cones have been brought out and placed across the pitch in the formation shown below.

Jog around the pitch by drawing a loop that visits every empty square, without visiting any square more than once. The loop must be made up of only horizontal and vertical lines, and cannot enter any square where there is a training cone. Instead of ranking your results, the boss has set a time limit for everyone to complete the course.

⏱ **Can you complete your loop in two minutes or less to score a penalty?**

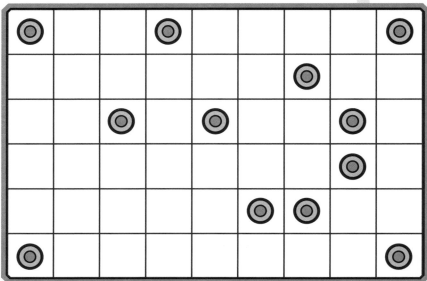

# INSIDE THE BOX

**Your team's earlier performance in the reaction-and-spacing exercise was pleasing. However, the manager's keen to make sure that the team are able to think on their feet – literally – so that they can make smart decisions on the pitch about positioning and play.**

As this is not a group that's used to training together week in, week out, the boss wants to try to create a team that are thinking as one, and able to keep an eye on the big picture while still picking up on the smaller details of the game.

The coaching staff have devised another tactical test to see how well the players are able to think outside the box – or in this case, inside the box. On the training pitch, they mark out the lines shown below and ask the whole squad to take a look at the playing area in front of them. They've drawn exactly enough rectangular zones on the pitch so that every player in the session can stand in the middle of a rectangle, with no players left over.

Your squad look around, sure that there are going to be some players left over at the end without a rectangle to stand in the middle of. This is a test of observation, however, so look more closely: how many rectangular zones can you see on the pitch in total, outlined in black? Assuming the manager's right and there are exactly as many rectangles as there are players, how many players are in the session in total? Don't forget to include the large rectangle all around the outside of the pitch itself.

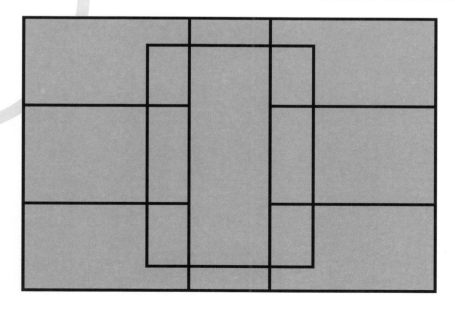

SOLUTION ON PAGE **181**

# PRECISE PERCEPTION

**When it comes to playing on the international stage, your team need to make sure they do not allow any avoidable errors to creep in. Even in the qualifiers, you need to be at the top of your game. In this exercise, you'll have your skills of observation tested so that when game time comes, you can be sure you're making footballing decisions based on what's really unfolding in front of you.**

Whichever goal the play is heading towards, your team need to be eagle-eyed and able to spot tiny changes in positioning among the opposition. If you're on the attack, you'll need to keep a close eye on the defence to make sure neither you, nor any team-mates you pass to, stray into an offside position. If you're defending – especially in the penalty area – your focus on the other team's positioning needs to be sharp and accurate. Not only is it essential for blocking any shots heading on target, but a misjudged tackle on an opposition player might cost you a penalty.

Your manager has set you a visual perception test ahead of your first qualifying match, to see how well you do at spotting subtle changes in the play around you: can you find ten differences between the two images opposite?

A pacy game is expected in this first round, so the boss wants to know you're able to make this type of observation under time pressure. To that end, time how long it takes you to find the first five differences before continuing, and rate your skills according to the scoreboard below.

## How did you score?

| ⏱ More than 5 minutes: You've been booked! | ⏱ 3-5 minutes: Slow spectator | ⏱ 2-3 minutes: Average observer | ⏱ 1-2 minutes: Eagle-eyed | ⏱ Less than 1 minute: Penalty scored! |
|---|---|---|---|---|

SOLUTION ON PAGE **181**

# DEFENSIVE MATCH

**This is the final training session before your first qualifying match tomorrow.**

Your manager is counting on you to guide the team through the games. For some of the team, it will be the first time they represent their country, and you want to make sure the basics are covered in case any nerves take over during the match.

Although the starting formation has already been decided and the players know their roles, the manager wants to make sure players can quickly regroup if they get out of position and return to the opponent they are marking. The players on the pitch below are, therefore, divided into two teams: one with orange bibs and one with blue. The aim of the game is to match up pairs of players – one of each bib colour – so that each player has one designated player of the opposite bib colour to mark.

Can you quickly demonstrate how the pairs of players should be matched up in the scenario below? Draw horizontal and vertical lines to join the players into pairs, so each pair contains one orange player and one blue player. Lines cannot cross either another line or a player.

# PITCH POSSESSION

**Your first World Cup qualifying match is here, and you're ready to take on the opposition. You proudly lead your team out on to the pitch.**

Now is the time to put your physical training and tactical analysis into practice on the international stage. The referee's whistle blows and the clock starts. Game on!

The first half of the match passes quickly and your team are playing well – those quick-thinking reaction skills are beginning to pay off. Just before the whistle blows for half-time, however, a gap opens up in the defence and the opposition manage to score: you're 1-0 down. Your manager wants to try to work out what went wrong, suspecting that not everyone in the team was in the right place at the right time. Can you create a possession map of the pitch below, showing the areas in which each player – represented by a number – has had possession of the ball?

Draw along some of the dashed grid lines to divide the pitch into a set of rectangles and/or squares, so that each shape contains exactly one number and every number is contained within a shape. The number in each shape must be equal to the number of squares contained in that shape. Each number represents one player in the team, and the size of the shape shows where they've had possession of the ball.

When the whole pitch is mapped out, take a look at the results. The striped area on the left is where the gap in the defence opened up and allowed the opposition to score. How many players are occupying this area? Work it out by counting the number of player areas that overlap or are contained within this striped section.

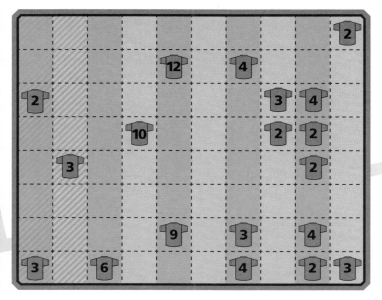

SOLUTION ON PAGE 182

# GOALSCORERS

**After a bit of a talking-to, your team are back out on the pitch for the second half. You need to score at least two goals in this half to win, and there's no room for more errors.**

Although it's not a knockout match, you can't really afford to lose a game so early on. Can your team overturn the 1–0 deficit and win their first qualifier?

Shown on the pitch below is an incomplete map of shots on target from both penalty areas in the second half of the match, overlaid on top of one another. Orange numbers represent your team's strikers, and blue numbers show the opposition. There are three goals scored in the second half – but which team fired them home?

Map out the individual shots on target by drawing a series of separate paths, each connecting a pair of identical numbers of the same colour. No more than one path can enter any grid square, and paths can only travel horizontally or vertically between squares. When a path crosses through a ball, it's a goal: if the path is between two orange numbers, it's a goal for your team; if it's a path between two blue numbers, however, it means the opposition have scored.

Can you map out all the shots to reveal the final score of the game?

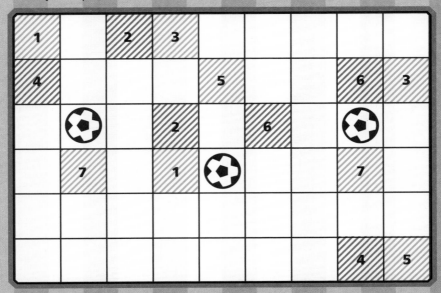

# WARM-UP

**You've made it through the first qualifier, but it wasn't the walk in the park you hoped it would be. However, the final result was nothing to be ashamed of.**

The second match isn't far off, and there's definitely room for improvement. In the warm-up exercise below, the whole squad have been called in for training, as your manager is still sizing up the team for the next game.

Every player and member of staff is given a different number from 1 to 54, and some of them are sent to stand out on the pitch, as shown below. Can you find a way of placing the rest of the players and staff evenly around the pitch so that a ball can be passed to every person exactly once?

Space out the people on the pitch so that each square contains a number from 1 to 54, and so that every player only touches the ball once – with no repeated numbers. Place the players so that the ball can be passed between all of them in increasing numerical order, starting with 1 and ending at 54. The ball can only travel one square at a time and can only be passed horizontally or vertically – no diagonal passes are allowed in this exercise.

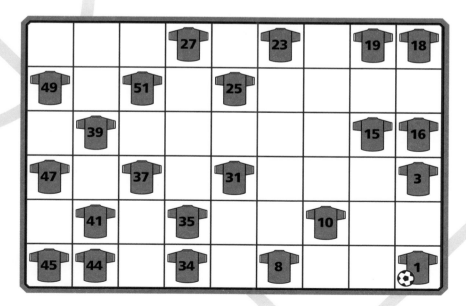

SOLUTION ON PAGE 182

# SET-PIECE PERCEPTION

After your first qualifier, the coaching team want to have a look at set pieces, making sure that you've sufficiently honed your skills in training before they crop up on the next matchday. Lining up for a free kick can be pretty nerve-racking – especially if you're having to defend it – so preparing in advance is important. In particular, your team need to be paying close attention to how the opposition are moving when the ball comes in. If you let them get away from you, they could create the perfect space to get up in the air and score.

Given that you're all pretty close together in the penalty box, you should be able to spot small changes in the other team's positioning that can tell you what they're going to attempt next. You can guarantee that they'll have practised their set pieces too and will likely have a tricky plan in place, so it's up to you to try to work out what they're up to – and ideally before they do it, so that you can intercept! It's time to test your powers of observation.

The players in the images opposite are all competing in the penalty area. There are a few subtle changes, however, between the two photos. Can you spot ten differences between picture A and picture B?

Once again, these observations should be made at speed, so set a timer when you start trying to spot the differences.

⏱ **Can you find them all in under three minutes to score a penalty?**

# DEFENCE DELEGATION

**It's back to the drawing board tactically, because your manager is unhappy about the way the defence broke up in the first half of your recent qualifying game.**

When you mapped out the possession stats from the match, it was clear that not everyone was occupying an equal amount of territory – with some players covering much more ground than others, errors were allowed to creep in. The boss is determined that you won't make the same mistake in the next match.

In the previous match, the four defenders didn't maintain their spacing evenly, and the opposition managed to slip through. Below is a rough sketch of half of the pitch, showing the portion of the field that the defenders should be occupying. Can you divide up the section of the pitch as shown to illustrate where each of the defenders should be focusing their attention, and make sure the whole area is covered equally?

Draw along some of the dashed grid lines in order to divide the pitch section into four regions – one for each defender to focus on. The regions should all be identical in size and shape, although they may be rotated (but not reflected) relative to one another.

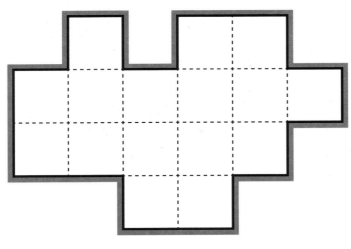

# SPEED-PASSING LOOP

Now that the team have a better idea of where they should be placed on the pitch, it's time to perfect some technical skills. Passing the ball to one another should be second nature, but it never hurts to practise! Short, accurate passes are harder for the opposition to intercept, and you want to make sure your team aren't needlessly wasting possession.

On the pitch below, each of the shirts shows a player on the training pitch. Can you find a way for the ball to be passed to every player in a loop, by drawing lines to connect the players to represent each pass between them?

All passes must be short, meaning they can only occur between two players who are immediately next to one another – and, again, only horizontal and vertical passes between players are allowed. The loop drawn to represent the passes cannot cross or touch itself at any point (some of the passes in the loop are already shown).

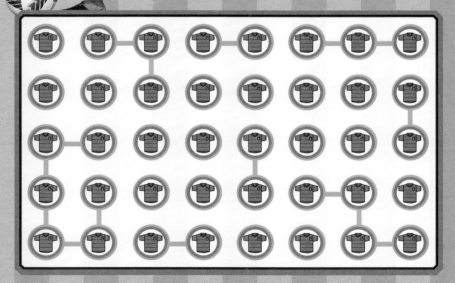

23

SOLUTION ON PAGE 183

# ON-FIELD OBSERVATION

High cross-field passes are a great way to get the ball advantageously to one of your own tall players. If you're able to deliver them accurately enough, they're less open to interception than passes drilled along the ground. That extra airtime also means that there's a little longer for your team to anticipate where the ball will wind up – but the same is true for the opposition. Your manager wants to make sure you're staying on top of your observation exercises, so that you can always make sure you're in the right position to receive the ball.

It's not always easy to judge a header, and moving just half an inch in the wrong direction might send the ball off on a very different trajectory. You also want to be able to carefully calculate the movement of the ball, and of the other players, so that you can wait until the opportune moment to make your move and take the defender marking you by surprise. The ability to read subtle changes in the play is the best way to calculate your plan of attack, so it's time to test your observation skills once again. In the images opposite, two players have jumped to get to the ball, both hoping to use the extra height to their advantage. Can you find ten differences between the two images?

The manager wants you to carry through the momentum from your speed-passing exercise, so this test of your perception should be timed. Set a stopwatch when you start to look for differences, and then stop when you've found them all. Compare your score against the scoreboard below – have you improved since your first visual perception test?

## How did you score?

| ⏱ More than 8 minutes: Card conceded! | ⏱ 6-8 minutes: Slow spectator | ⏱ 4-6 minutes: Average observer | ⏱ 2-4 minutes: Eagle-eyed | ⏱ Less than 2 minutes: Penalty scored! |
|---|---|---|---|---|

# PENALTY-BOX POSITIONING

**The second qualifier is approaching fast. Before the game begins, the manager pulls you into a final tactics session to make sure that lessons have been learned from the first match in terms of defensive positioning.**

It's essential for the whole team to be able to react quickly and correct themselves if a similar situation arises where gaps open up in the formation. In particular, though, the boss wants to know that you, as captain, can take a look at the players' positions and quickly communicate any necessary adjustments to the team.

The coaching staff have come up with a scenario for you below, mapped out on an area roughly covering the penalty box. They want to see how fast you can fill the hypothetical gaps without letting your own side, or the opposition, dominate a particular area of the box. In this case, your team are shown with a blue shirt, and the opposition with an orange shirt. Place a blue or orange shirt in every empty cell so that there is an equal number of each colour in every row and every column. Reading along a row or column, there may be no more than two of the same colour in succession.

How fast can you fill the box and make sure the teams are balanced in their positioning throughout the playing area? Time yourself as you fill out the box, and then compare your score against the ratings shown below.

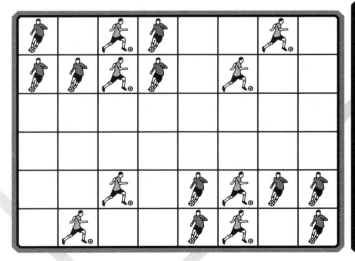

## How did you score?

⏱ More than 5 minutes: That's a card!

⏱ 3-5 minutes: Average observer

⏱ 2-3 minutes: Rapid reporter

⏱ Less than 2 minutes: Penalty scored!

# OPPORTUNITIES

**It's the second qualifier and your team are ready for the challenge. The manager is happy that you've got what it takes to lead the team to victory again – and ideally, this time, without conceding any goals.**

The opposition won the coin toss, and they'll be kicking off first. You're all in your starting positions – and the whistle blows!

The match is off to a great start and both teams are full of energy, so you'll need to keep up the pace if you want to outlast the opposition. Towards the end of the first half, you make a great interception, which gives you a chance to set up a goalscoring opportunity. You take a look at the field in front of you to see who's in the best position to receive the ball and take it towards goal.

Each of the numbered shirts below represents a player, where orange shirts are your team and blue are the opposition. To work out who has the best availability, draw one or more horizontal or vertical lines travelling away from each player to show their coverage of the pitch. Each player's number tells you how many grid squares their lines travel to, although the player squares themselves do not count toward this total. Lines shouldn't enter or cross over squares containing other players, nor enter a square containing a line coming from another player. When you are finished, every non-player square will have a line in it. All the lines coming out of the player numbered 7 have been drawn in to show you how it works.

You want to pass the ball so that it lands where the ball is shown on the field, since, if one of your players picks it up there, they're sure to score. According to your drawn lines, which player will be able to reach it?

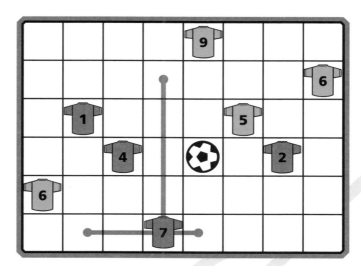

SOLUTION ON PAGE **184**

# FINAL WHISTLE

**Your composure and quick thinking mean you've delivered the ball to the correct player – and opened the scoring!**

The rest of the first half passes without much incident, but your team are beginning to look tired, so you're pleased to be a goal up when the half-time whistle blows. After what feels like far too short a break in the dressing room, you're back out on the pitch for the second half – and this time, you feel confident there are a *lot* more goals on the way.

The team appear refreshed after the break, but you decide it's time to put those passing skills into action so that the players aren't running themselves into exhaustion. The image of the pitch on the opposite page shows some of the tactical passes made by both teams in the final minutes of the second half, during which several goals were scored, among a host of shots from both teams. Can you map out all of the passes that took place, and find out how many goals each team scored?

Each of the numbered shirts opposite represents a player. Join pairs of numbers with up to two horizontal or vertical lines, with each line representing the ball being passed once between players. Each player must have as many lines connected to them as specified by the shirt value, and no passes may cross. The finished layout must connect all players with lines, so the ball can travel between any pair of players by following one or more of the pass lines. Any lines that pass through orange stars are goals scored for your team, while lines that pass through a blue star mean you've conceded a goal.

Precision passing is the aim of the game and, as the whistle blows, you find out if your plan was a good one. Have a look at the result on the pitch. How many goals did each team score, and what's the final score in the match, given that you were 1-0 up at half-time?

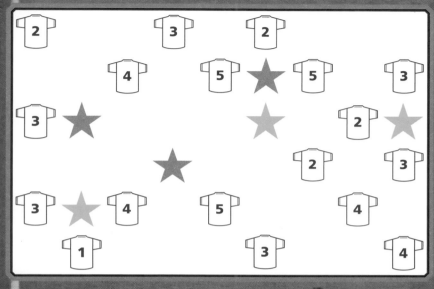

# BALL TRACKING

**Congratulations! The decision to focus on precision passing was a good one, and you've won your second qualifier.**

Your manager is happy that the defensive line held up this time, although a clean sheet would've been an added bonus. You want to take a closer look during training at how some of the opposition's mistakes could have been turned into goalscoring opportunities for your team. In particular, you want to focus on anticipating the opposition's movements so that you have a better chance of making key interceptions. Take a look at the scenario below. Can you show how the player marked A will try to get the ball to the position marked B?

The other players in shaded boxes indicate areas protected by defenders in

your team who, for the purposes of this exercise, don't move. Join some pairs of neighbouring circles with horizontal and vertical lines to make a single path that travels from A to B, and which does not touch or cross itself at any point (nor branch off into a dead-end path). Numbers outside the pitch specify the number of circles in their row or column that are visited by the path. (Player A's starting position and the ball B are included in those numbers.) The path cannot cross over any of the defenders.

|  | 4 | 4 | 4 | 2 | 1 | 1 |
|---|---|---|---|---|---|---|
| 3 | ○ | ○ | ○ | ○ | ○ | ○ |
| 3 | A | ○ | ○ | [defender] | ○ | ○ |
| 4 | ○ | ○ | ○ | ○ | ○ | [defender] |
| 6 | ○ | ○ | ○ | ○ | ○ | B |

# ZONAL MARKING

**Following on from the last training session, your manager thinks it's key that you focus on improving anticipation, reading the opposition's movement and using it to your advantage to try to interrupt their play.**

The next team you will face are famous for their rigid zone defence, although their starting formations tend to be a little unconventional.

In the tactics session, your manager wants the team to try to get their heads around the upcoming opposition's unusual positioning style. The coaching staff have created a map of the opposition's most commonly used formation, shown below, but want you to put the finishing touches to it yourself, so that the whole team can see how it fits together. Fortunately, they've given you a few clues. Can you use them to map out the zones you should expect to find each of the opposition players in?

Draw along some of the dashed lines to divide the grid into a set of zones, each containing one of every letter from the word "ZONE". Each area, when it is completed, is a defensive zone, which will be covered by one of the opposition players in your upcoming match.

| E | O | Z | Z | O | N | Z | E |
|---|---|---|---|---|---|---|---|
| N | E | N | O | E | N | N | O |
| O | Z | N | O | N | N | Z | Z |
| E | N | O | E | E | E | O | E |
| Z | Z | E | N | Z | O | N | Z |
| Z | N | O | O | Z | E | O | E |

SOLUTION ON PAGE **185**

# ANTICIPATION CHECK

**Even in these qualifying rounds, all of the teams are putting in their best efforts, which means relentless, pacy football that's full of energy. As a result, it can be hard to keep track of every player during the game – and whether each player is in the position they're supposed to be. If you're defending the ball in the opposition's half, you need to keep a sharp eye on the players in both teams, to make sure there are no gaps opening up that the opposition can take advantage of.**

As the team captain, you need to be the definitive on-field authority, so it's important for your observation and attention skills to be up to scratch in case you need to put anyone from your own team in their place. Like everyone else, you want to make sure you've left it all out on the pitch, so you can't afford to leave room for mistakes, however small. You should be better able to predict the other players' movements if you watch their positioning very carefully.

In the busy penalty box opposite, players from both teams are clearly keeping a close eye on the ball. There are ten subtle differences between the two images, however, and it's up to you to find them. Can you spot all the changes?

Your manager wants you to prove that you can pass this test under the time pressure, so time yourself as you spot the changes.

🕐 **Can you find them all in four minutes or less to score a penalty?**

# INDIRECT ROUTES

**In most of the training sessions so far, you've been focusing on covering the whole pitch, whether for a fitness test or in team exercises involving the whole squad.**

In this session, you'll still be covering a lot of the field, but you'll need to think a little more about your route around it. In the face of aggressive marking, sometimes you'll have to travel with the ball a little further than you might like – and possibly even away from the direction of play you were aiming for. In order to hold off and get around assertive defenders, you should be ready to take a more indirect route.

Each number on the pitch below represents one player from the opposing team, and the value of the number tells you how closely they tend to mark other players: a higher number means a more assertive style of defence. Can you create a loop around the pitch that shows how the various defenders might force your path if you approach with the ball?

Draw a single loop that passes through some of the empty squares on the pitch, using only horizontal and vertical lines. Plan your route carefully, since the loop cannot re-enter any square. The loop must start on the player shown and pass through the given number of touching squares next to each numbered opposition player, including diagonally touching squares.

# CROSS-FIELD PASSING

**It's the final training session before the last qualifying match. Confident that your short-passing game is accurate, it's time to test longer cross-field passes. Your manager doesn't want to see any passes of this length drilled across the ground – they're wide open to interception, and you don't want to give the opposing team any chances.**

In this session, you'll practise making airborne passes so that they curve neatly over the heads of defenders, and right into a dangerous position in front of your players. Or, at least, that's the plan!

On the pitch below, the ball needs to be passed between each of the pairs of players with identical numbers, with lines to indicate the route of each pass. Passes can travel horizontally, vertically or diagonally through the middle of empty squares. No more than one line can enter any square, but lines *can* cross if they do so diagonally on the join between four squares. Can you map out all of the cross-field passes?

When you're done, take a look at all the paths. There are five passes overall – but how many of these cross-field passes crossed one another in the session?

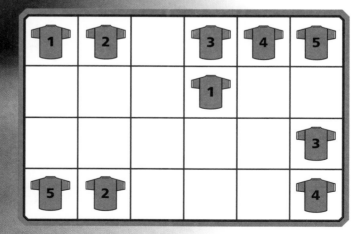

SOLUTION ON PAGE **186**

# BREAKTHROUGH LINES

**It's nearly time for your last qualifying match, but first it's a final tactics session. Your manager is now pleased with the team's level of fitness, and the squad have come a long way since the first qualifier.**

You've learned from your defensive mistakes and improved your awareness of your team-mates' positioning on the pitch.

Your manager has one final scenario to explore with the team. In the first match, the coaching staff were impressed (and a little annoyed) by the way the opposition were able to cleanly break through the defence and create a clear line for a goalscoring opportunity. In this final session, they want each player to attempt to create a similarly direct, "route-one" passage of play straight through the opposition's defensive zones. The aim is for all the players to visualise a direct line between themselves and the goal, and then mark out the path they should run to give themselves an unopposed opening to score.

The boss has mapped out some hypothetical defensive zones on the pitch below for the players to find a clear way through, and wants you, the captain, to make the first attempt.

The bold lines each mark out a defensive zone that needs to be broken through. Draw a loop that visits every square only once, travelling only horizontally or vertically between squares. In addition, the loop can only enter and exit each bold-lined defensive region once – so there's no going back on yourself.

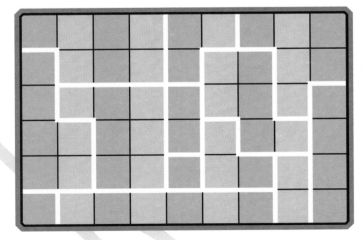

# IN TOUCH

**The final qualifier has begun! If you and the team win this match, you'll be heading to the group stage in style.**

Given that you've already won two matches, you can go through with a draw, but you'd like to keep up the winning momentum. In spite of your tactical efforts, the play is scrappy. In fact, hoofing the ball into the stands seems to be the main method of defence, and that means there are plenty of set pieces for both sides.

On the pitch below is an incomplete map of some of the corners, throw-ins and goal kicks that have been awarded during the first half. Three of them have resulted in goals, marked by the three footballs on the pitch. Work out which team scored each of these goals by drawing a series of separate paths, each connecting a pair of identical numbers on identical-coloured shirts. Paths are drawn by joining neighbouring square centres with horizontal or vertical lines. No more than one path can enter any cell.

The throw-ins came from the touchlines, so paths may run off one side of the pitch. If so, the same path will continue on the opposite side of the pitch. This allows paths to "wrap around" from one side of the pitch to the other. When a path crosses through a ball, it's a goal: if the path is between two orange shirts, it's a goal for your team; if it's between two blue shirts, it means the opposition have scored.

⏱ **When the whistle blows for half-time, what's the score? Figure it out in under three minutes to score a penalty.**

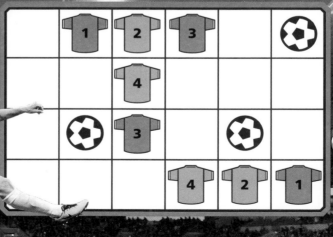

SOLUTION ON PAGE **187**

# PLAYMAKER

**The mood in the dressing room at half-time isn't ideal. Your manager is frustrated at the lack of discipline and the absence on the pitch of the tactical play you've discussed at length. Can you inspire your players to rediscover the skills you've been working so hard on in your training and tactics sessions, and lead them to victory in the second half?**

Heading back out on to the pitch after the hairdryer treatment, you try to recall the training sessions since the second qualifier. You're not sure that you'll be able to make a clean break through the opposition like your manager hoped – the other team are pressing and marking tightly, making it difficult even to pass the ball. Luckily, your manager has prepared you for this and demonstrated how a longer, well-planned route around defenders can sometimes be the key to success.

Can you create an indirect path that allows you to keep possession of the ball and work your way around the defenders to score at least one more goal for your team? To do so, make your way from the goal area on the left to the goal on the right – which is the one you're aiming for – without crossing any of the blue lines in the maze. If your path crosses through an orange ball, you've scored a goal; if it passes through a blue ball, the opposition have scored. You may not retrace your path at any point.

When you reach the other side, the final whistle blows. What is the full-time score, given that you were losing 2-1 at half-time?

# THE GROUP STAGE

After a promising start in the qualifiers, the team are ready for their next big challenge.

During this stage, there are three games to play and, just as in the qualifying rounds, there's time in between each game for training and tactics sessions. You'll need to win at least two of your games to get through to the knockout rounds, as only the top two in each group will advance. After a disappointing draw in the final qualifying match, you know that both the management and the players will be looking for a clean sweep on the way through to the next stage to prove they have what it takes to lift the trophy.

So, lace up your boots and head over to the training pitch for your first warm-up!

# RUNNING DRILLS

**In this first session, you'll be using some of the skills you've honed in previous warm-ups to create a running loop around the training pitch that visits each square exactly once.**

This time, however, there's a new twist – literally. The manager has come up with a way of making sure that your route is full of twists and turns, in order to test both your agility and your ability to quickly change your direction, even when running at full speed.

   Draw the running loop on the image below, using only horizontal and vertical lines to move from square to square, and make sure that every *second* turn in your loop is in a square marked with a training cone. So, in other words, you'll alternate between turning in a square *without* a cone and turning in a square *with* a cone.

   This is also a test of fitness, so the manager wants each of the team members to complete the exercise as fast as possible. Once you're ready to begin drawing the route, start a timer and only stop it once you've joined up the final sections and obeyed all of the turning cones. Then compare your time against the scoreboard opposite to see how you're shaping up.

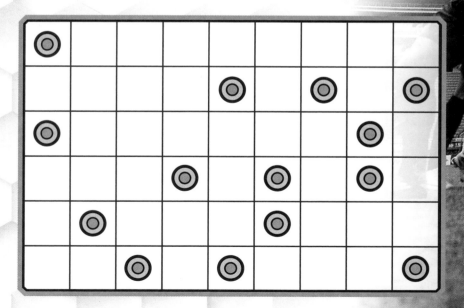

**How did you do?**

| ⏱ Over 10 minutes: You're booked! | ⏱ 8-10 minutes: Sloppy sprinter | ⏱ 6-8 minutes: Average athlete | ⏱ 4-6 minutes: Nifty negotiator | ⏱ Under 4 minutes: Penalty scored! |

# THINKING TOGETHER

In the qualifying rounds, the coaching staff spent a lot of time sharpening the players' mental fitness. They focused on testing their observation skills to make sure that the team could pick up on the opposition's tactics and pre-empt their next moves. Now that you're in the group stage, it's more important than ever that the whole team are aware of the wider game, and no individuals are getting too tangled up in their own play.

In short, your manager wants to make sure you're all working together mentally, as well as physically. A team that think together, win together.

Your manager has come up with an exercise to see how well you pick up on the clues given out by all of the players on the pitch – not just your own team – to help anticipate how the play is going to unfold. On the page opposite is an image of a crucial moment in a match, with one big difference: the ball has been removed. Can you work out, from the positions and eyelines of the players shown, where the ball would be at the moment when the photo was taken?

Work out which square in the grid you think the ball should be in, and then make a note of that square's coordinates. Once you're done, see how well you did by comparing your choice against the scoreboard below, depending on how close you were to the answer shown in the solutions. Trace a path from your square to the ball's real position, first with a horizontal line and then a vertical one. Then count how many squares – if any – are between your solution and the correct one.

## How did you score?

| 4 squares away: Another booking! | 2-3 squares away: Sloppy spectator | 1 square away: Eagle-eyed | Right on target: Penalty scored! |
| --- | --- | --- | --- |

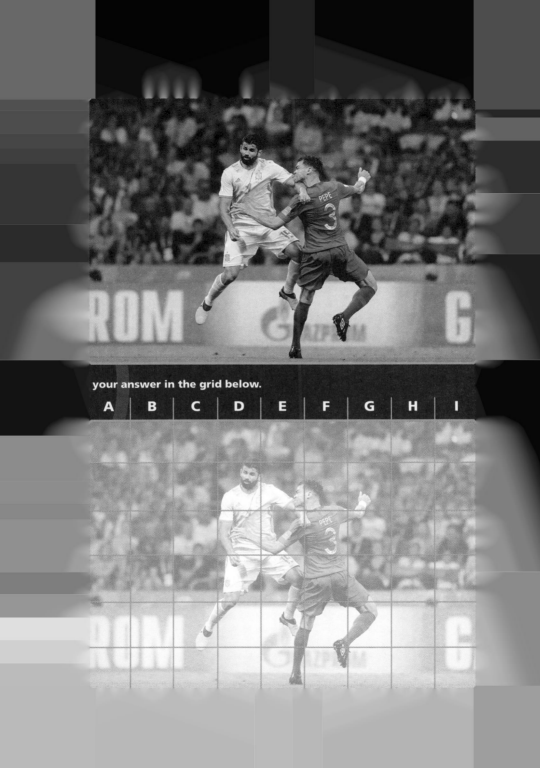

your answer in the grid below.

| A | B | C | D | E | F | G | H | I |

# STAR SCORER

**After your first training session, it's back to the tactics sheet. Your manager was generally pleased with the group's performances in qualifying, and it's clear that the players are confident about which zones they should each be covering at different times.**

The problem is that tunnel vision seems to be affecting some of your team-mates. They are focusing too much on their own game, not taking in the subtle clues on the pitch that reveal what the opposition are about to do, and thus letting players ghost past them.

Your manager wants the whole team to improve their observation skills to try to get ahead of the game. In the final qualifying match, the opposition were able to put away two goals in quick succession, as your team didn't spot their star striker racing up the pitch and creating goalscoring chances.

On the board below, your manager has sketched out a portion of the pitch and wants each player in the team, as quickly as possible, to point out the hidden star striker.

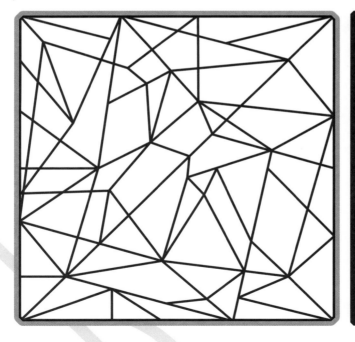

How quickly can you find this five-pointed star hidden in the picture? Do it in under 30 seconds to score a penalty. Bear in mind that the scale or angle might be different compared to the star shown.

# CIRCUIT TRAINING

**It's easy enough to spot individual players when you're standing still, but what about when you're moving around?**

The key to this next exercise is multitasking, and it tests how well you keep an eye on a number of unfolding situations around the pitch. Your manager splits the squad into three teams and gives each team a different route around the pitch. In total, the three loops cover the whole pitch, and cross paths with one another several times. Some of each loop segment is shown on the pitch below, but can you complete all three looped routes simultaneously? Any segments you draw out for one loop will have implications for the other two.

Draw a set of three loops that together pass through all the squares on the

pitch. In each square, a loop may pass straight through, turn 90 degrees, or cross directly over another loop segment. Apart from in "crossing squares", only one loop may enter any one square. Lines can never be drawn diagonally. Each loop must pass through at least one shirt, and all shirts containing the same number must be part of the same loop and no other. You cannot add extra lines to any of the squares in which fragments are already given.

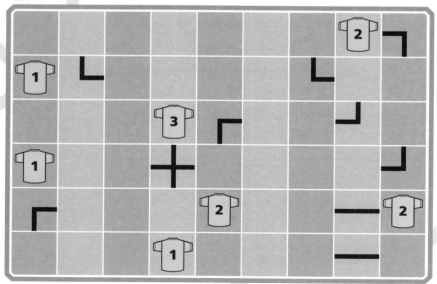

SOLUTION ON PAGE **189**

# THE ART OF FLICK-ONS

**After a mind-boggling multi-loop workout, you turn your focus to some of the finer details of the game.**

It's time to work on headers from set pieces. You and your team-mates will be trying to head each ball so that it turns its path by exactly 90 degrees (a right-angled turn). In the example below, a ball travelling down towards the player (marked by a red line below) should be headed so that it travels away from them at the angle shown.

On the pitch below, some of the squad are ready to kick the ball into play. They have been sorted into pairs, and each pair labelled with an identical number/letter combination. The objective is to make sure that the ball can be kicked in from one side of the pitch and deflected neatly by a given number of headers so that it reaches the player with the same label as the original kicker.

**PLAYER** → **DIRECTION OF BALL**

Draw diagonal lines across certain squares to indicate players, with exactly one player per bold-lined region. The players must be placed so that a ball kicked into the grid from each lettered clue would then exit the grid at the same letter elsewhere, having been deflected by the exact number of players indicated by the number next to the letter.

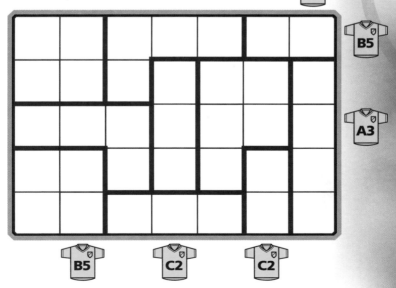

A3

B5

A3

B5    C2    C2

# SIDELINES

**Your first group match is tomorrow, but the manager still thinks there is some tactical fine-tuning to do. Now that you've practised deft deflections on the pitch, the next step is to see whether players on the sidelines can quickly calculate whom they should send the ball to when set pieces arise.**

A well-placed throw-in near the box can be as useful as a free kick – if the thrower takes time to find the right recipient.

  The manager has sketched out a map of the penalty box below and wants you to place a player into each empty square until the box is filled. In this case, the players should be represented by a digit from 1 to 6, and you should place each digit just once into every row and column. Values outside the grid give the total of the digits in the indicated diagonals.

  When the grid is complete, take a look at the yellow arrows, which show four directions that the ball might be thrown in from the sideline. If you now imagine that your team members are indicated by those squares containing even digits, and the opposition by those with odd digits, whoever is taking the throw-in would want to make sure they're throwing to an even-numbered player. Which of the four arrows – A, B, C or D – points to a diagonal that contains only even numbers?

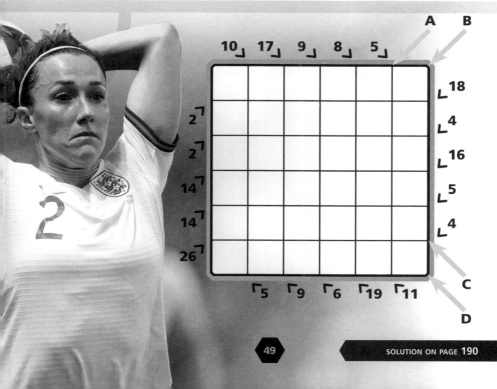

SOLUTION ON PAGE **190**

# INDIRECT FREE KICK

**It's game time! The first match of the group stage has arrived, and you're keen to execute on your training skills.**

After the whistle blows, the first ten minutes of the game seem evenly matched. The opposition are a little too aggressive and, after they impede the progress of one of your players, you're awarded an indirect free kick from a great position just outside the box. You've been chosen to take the kick and, as it is indirect, it must touch another player before a goal can be scored. It's time to put your heading training into action!

Map out the locations of the various players in the box below and work out who is best placed to receive the ball from you. Place A, B and C once each into every row and column within the grid, with each letter representing one player. A player labelled A is most likely to score from your kick, while a player labelled C is least likely to score. Each given letter outside the grid must match the closest letter to it in the same row/column. Letters may not share squares, and there will, therefore, always be one empty square in every row and column.

When you've placed all the letters, look at the arrows indicating your options for the indirect free kick. You want to kick the ball directly to a player labelled A without going over anyone's head. Which arrow represents the way you should aim the free kick?

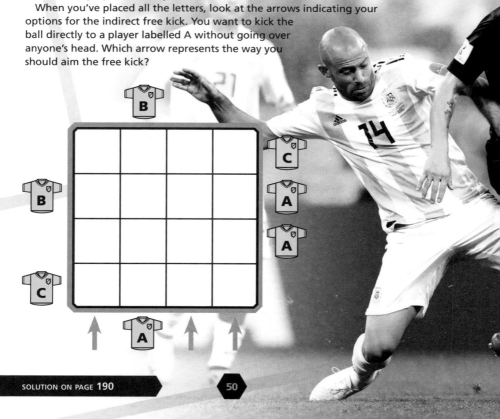

# VAR

**At half-time, you're pleased with your players: the score is 1-0 to you, after your success with the early indirect free kick. Even though you haven't scored any more goals, you've so far kept a clean sheet and you're confident you can hold them off.**

The second half passes and in extra time the score is still 1-0. Just before the final whistle, one of your forwards takes a powerful shot at goal, but the ball hits the crossbar. It looks like it's in, as it bounces straight downward and apparently into the goal, before bouncing back out again. The referee initially disallows the goal, but VAR is called in to see if the ball did, indeed, cross the line. Can you use the clues below to work out whether the goal should be allowed or not?

Shade some cells by obeying the clue constraints at the start of each row or column. The clues provide, in reading order, the length of every run of consecutive shaded cells in each row and column. There must be a gap of at least one empty cell between each run of shaded cells in the same row or column.

The finished puzzle will reveal a simple picture which shows the goal line and the ball at its furthest position toward the goal. In this image, the area to the bottom right of the line is inside the goal. For the goal to be allowed, the whole of the ball must be over the whole of the line.

Take a look at the completed image. Should the goal be allowed or not?

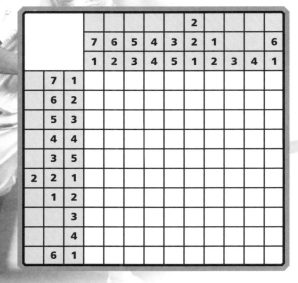

| | | | | | | | 2 | | | | |
|---|---|---|---|---|---|---|---|---|---|---|---|
| | | 7 | 6 | 5 | 4 | 3 | 2 | 1 | | | 6 |
| | | 1 | 2 | 3 | 4 | 5 | 1 | 2 | 3 | 4 | 1 |
| 7 | 1 | | | | | | | | | | |
| 6 | 2 | | | | | | | | | | |
| 5 | 3 | | | | | | | | | | |
| 4 | 4 | | | | | | | | | | |
| 3 | 5 | | | | | | | | | | |
| 2 | 2 | 1 | | | | | | | | | |
| 1 | 2 | | | | | | | | | | |
| | 3 | | | | | | | | | | |
| | 4 | | | | | | | | | | |
| 6 | 1 | | | | | | | | | | |

51

SOLUTION ON PAGE 190

# QUICK LOOP

**After a clean sheet and an energetic first match of the full competition, it's back to the training ground for another session.**

The coaching team are feeling generous after your recent victory, so they've set the squad a simple warm-up task that you should be familiar with.

Dribble the ball around the pitch by drawing a loop from the player that visits every white square, without visiting any square more than once. Your loop must be made up only of horizontal and vertical lines, and cannot enter any squares where there are training cones.

Of course, it's not all plain sailing – this is going to be another test of speed. When you begin the loop, start a timer, and stop when you've drawn in the final section. Take a look at your time and compare it against the scoreboard below to track your progress.

### How did you score?

| ⏱ More than 4 minutes: That's a booking! | ⏱ 3-4 minutes: Lagging behind | ⏱ 2-3 minutes: Slow and steady | ⏱ 1-2 minutes: Speedy striker | ⏱ Less than 1 minute: Penalty scored! |

# FIND THE DEFENDERS

**Your manager is pleased with the way the team played in the first group-stage match, especially as the training in the build-up proved very useful – headers and ball-placement calculations were used to great effect when they were needed most.**

In this session, the boss wants to look at anticipating the opposition's movements and encourage the team to think ahead, to make sure they don't miss opportunities to burst past a stodgy defence.

Hidden in the grid below are several defenders, lurking in some of the empty squares. Can you work out where they all are from the clues you have been given?

Place defenders into some of the empty squares in the grid. Each square containing a number tells you the number of touching squares that have defenders in them – including diagonally touching squares. No more than one defender may be placed per square. How many hidden defenders are there in total?

| 1 | 2 |   | 2 |   |   |
|---|---|---|---|---|---|
|   |   | 4 |   |   | 2 |
|   |   |   | 2 | 3 |   |
|   | 1 | 2 |   |   |   |

SOLUTION ON PAGE **191**

# DRIBBLING DRILLS

**Now that you've practised keeping an eye out for defenders, it's time to work out how to play against them.**

In this session, you'll be tested on how well you can work your way around some of the pitch while keeping the ball close to you, and preventing the marked defenders from taking possession of the ball.

Training cones have been set out on the pitch opposite, as well as several squad players wearing numbered bibs – they're acting as the opposition's defenders.

Create a loop by dribbling the ball around the defenders, connecting some of the cones to do so. Cones can only be joined by horizontal or vertical lines, and each cone can be visited no more than once. Connect your loop so that each numbered defender is surrounded by the number of line segments specified by their bib.

As you're passing by each defender, you'll have to keep the ball close to your feet, to make sure it's not open to interception. What's more, completing your loop at speed should help you keep possession. How quickly can you complete it? Compare your time to the scoreboard opposite to see how you did.

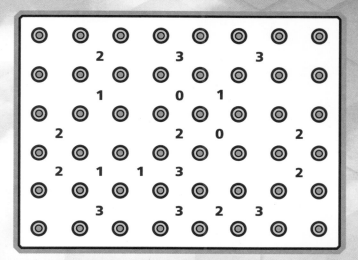

# MISSING SOMETHING

Although you and the team have trained well for set pieces, it's impossible to predict how a game will really play out until the match kicks off. When you're defending a set piece like a corner, there can be so many people in the box that it's hard enough to work out where the ball is, let alone how to get it to a place of safety. It's important for you and your players to be able to keep your cool and stay alert in the penalty area to avoid letting the ball out of your sight.

Your manager wants you to practise your observation skills – after all, you can't take proper advantage of a corner if you can't keep track of the ball. You'll need to be prepared for players blocking your sight line, either by moving in front of you or by jumping an inch higher. The same is true whether you're attacking or defending: it's always a useful skill to be able to spot the ball!

With that in mind, the manager has come up with an attention-based exercise for you. The photo opposite was taken during a set piece, and each of the players is reacting to the location of the ball – which has been removed from the image. Can you work out, from the positions and eyelines of the players shown, where the ball would be at the moment when the photo was taken?

Work out which square in the grid you think the ball should be in, and then make a note of that square's coordinates. Once you're done, see how well you did by comparing your choice against the scoreboard below, depending on how close you were to the answer shown in the solutions. Trace a path from your square to the ball's real position, first with a horizontal line and then a vertical one. Then count how many squares – if any – are between your solution and the correct one.

| How did you score? | | | | |
|---|---|---|---|---|
| 4+ squares away: Another booking! | 3 squares away: Slow spectator | 2 squares away: Average observer | 1 square away: Eagle-eyed | Right on target: Penalty scored! |

your answer in the grid below.

| A | B | C | D | E | F | G | H | I |

# OFFENSIVE DEFENCE

**It's the last tactics session before your second game of the group stage, and your final preparations are under way.**

While you've been focused on keeping possession in your training sessions, you need to prepare for the inevitable – that is, the opposition getting the ball!

Your manager has devised a way for the team to think about the opposition's possession, so that you can act quickly and prevent the other team from creating any goalscoring opportunities. The objective is to ensure that the opposition are never allowed more than six touches of the ball in a row – so, if they're on touch number six, it's time to get in, intercept the ball and break up their momentum.

On the sketch below, your manager has drawn out a map of hypothetical possession for different areas of the pitch, numbering the touches in each area of possession from 1 to 6. Can you separate out the areas by drawing along some of the dashed grid lines, creating areas that contain each of the numbers 1 to 6 exactly once?

| 4 | 2 | 6 | 3 | 5 | 1 | 5 | 6 |
|---|---|---|---|---|---|---|---|
| 5 | 2 | 6 | 3 | 3 | 1 | 4 | 2 |
| 3 | 6 | 6 | 1 | 5 | 2 | 4 | 1 |
| 1 | 4 | 2 | 4 | 5 | 3 | 4 | 5 |
| 1 | 4 | 5 | 1 | 3 | 4 | 2 | 2 |
| 3 | 6 | 2 | 1 | 3 | 6 | 5 | 6 |

# LOOP LOGISTICS

**Your second match of the group stage is tomorrow, and you're eager to build on the success of your first game.**

The squad has benefited from the intense training in the meantime and, hopefully, they'll be able to put their work on anticipation and reading the opposition to good use in the match.

This final training session is all about solidifying the basics. You'll take the ball around the pitch, choosing a route that keeps the opposition where you can see them, without giving them a chance to dispossess you.

Dribble the ball in a single loop using only horizontal and vertical lines between squares. Your loop must not cross or overlap itself and can only visit empty grid squares. Squares containing opposition players are marked with numbers, which indicate how many touching squares the loop passes through, including diagonally touching squares.

There are some mental obstacles to tackle in this exercise, but the coaching team are still treating it as a test of speed to make sure you're match fit for tomorrow. Can you complete the whole loop in under five minutes, starting and ending with the player shown? If so, mark a penalty scored by you at the back of the book.

| 2 | | | 4 | | | 4 | | |
|---|---|---|---|---|---|---|---|---|
| | | | | | | | | |
| | | | | | 5 | | | |
| | | | | | ⚽ | | 3 | |
| | | 4 | 2 | | | | | |
| | | | | | | | | |

SOLUTION ON PAGE **192**

# TOUCHLINE INSTRUCTIONS

**It's match day again, and you're looking forward to the challenge. Your opponents won all of their qualifying matches – and their opening group match – so you're facing a team in great form.**

The whistle blows and play is energetic from the off. The opposition are speedy and you'll need to think fast to keep up. The coaching staff are shouting at you from the sidelines, and you've got to work hard to try to understand what their instructions mean for your plan. Can you follow their advice and work out how they want you to dribble the ball from A to B below, without being intercepted by the opposition?

Shade in some squares to form a single possession route from A to B. It must be a route of touching squares that does not branch off or cross over itself. You cannot return to a square touching any earlier part of your route – not even diagonally. The coaching staff's clues are indicated by numbers outside the grid, with each clue specifying the number of squares in its row or column that are visited by the route, including the squares labelled A and B. The route can only move horizontally or vertically from square to touching square.

If your path enters a square marked in green, the opposition have managed to intercept you on your route. Do they intercept you or not?

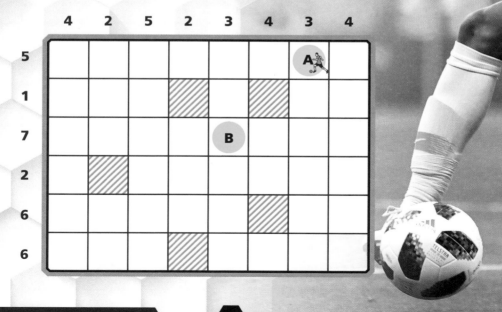

# ODDS AND EVENS

**After a disappointing first half, your team are behind when the whistle blows for half-time.**

As you catch your breath in the changing room, your manager reassures you that this is the best team you've played against so far and that, therefore, it's natural to be feeling the pressure at this stage. As you head out for the second half, you're hoping you can reverse your team's luck and pull through with a victory.

TThe second half is just as frantic as the first and, after 15 minutes, your team are exhausted. Unfortunately, there's a lot of work to do – and there are more goals on the way. Both teams are fighting hard for possession, and it's tough to keep track of the ball. Can you map out the directions of play in the grid below and work out which players managed to score in the second half?

Add numbers to the grid so that every square contains a number, and each number from 1 to 24 appears exactly once. Every number must be placed in a square whose arrow points in the direction of the next highest number.

Your team's possession is shown with even numbers, and the opposition's with odd numbers. Boxes shaded in green mark the points where a goal is scored: if the number in a box is even, it is a goal for your team; if it's odd, you've conceded a goal.

When all the numbers are placed, which team scored more goals? Given that you were 1-0 down at half-time, what's the final score in the match?

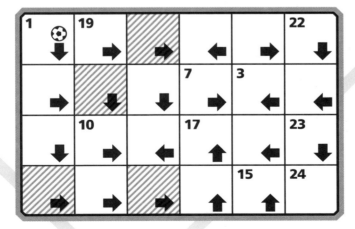

# MAN-MARKING

**Your team have suffered their first proper setback, and the players are understandably disappointed as you head back into training for the final match of the group stage.**

As things stand, you can still get out of your group by winning your next match – you would come second and thus be able to proceed to the knockout stage. As a team, you decide it's time to put defeat behind you and focus on the way forward.

In this exercise, your manager wants to try a new approach to defence. Instead of marking out specific zones for each player to try to stay within, the plan is to explore man-to-man marking a little more. Marking a player instead of a zone can be tiring stuff, but the boss thinks it might be the key to staying on top of the opposition in the upcoming match.

The squad have been split into two teams: one with yellow bibs and one with green. Yellow bibs, in this game, represent the opposition. Your team-mates have all strayed from the player they're meant to mark, and need to make it back into position quickly. As captain, you've got to work out which player they each need to run back to, and in which direction. Can you match up each yellow player with one green player, using only straight lines to join them? Lines cannot cross either another line or a player, and can only be placed horizontally or vertically.

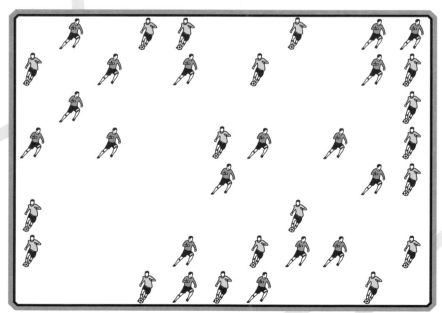

SOLUTION ON PAGE **193**

# QUICK OBSERVATION

When you're in the penalty area, quick reactions are a must – whether you're attacking or defending. In front of your own goal, it's crucial that you stay sharp and keep your eye on the unfolding situation to ensure you can successfully block any attempts on goal before they reach the keeper. When you're on the attack, speedy reflexes and sharp observations will mean you can take advantage of any errors the other team make, and turn their mistakes into goals.

In your previous game, your manager was disappointed with a lack of focus in the second half, which cost your team the match. The staff want to make sure that you're mentally ready for the next game, and that includes testing your attention to detail – you should be able to quickly read the scenario on the pitch and make any adjustments to your team's tactics.

With that in mind, the coach has devised another observation exercise for you. The players in the top image opposite are in a sticky situation, and there's a stray ball in the penalty area, dangerously close to the goal. The ball, however, has been removed from the image.

Work out which square in the grid you think the ball should be in, and then make a note of that square's coordinates. Once you're done, see how well you did by comparing your choice against the scoreboard below, depending on how close you were to the answer shown in the solutions. Trace a path from your square to the ball's real position, first with a horizontal line and then a vertical one. Then count how many squares – if any – are between your solution and the correct one.

| **How did you score?** | | | | |
|---|---|---|---|---|
| 4+ squares away: Another booking! | 3 squares away: Sloppy spectator | 2 squares away: Average observer | 1 square away: Eagle-eyed | Right on target: Penalty scored! |

your answer in the grid below.

| A | B | C | D | E | F | G | H | I |
|---|---|---|---|---|---|---|---|---|

# TIGHT BLOCKING

**It's your final training session and the coaching staff want to see you combine some of the techniques that you've been working on up until now.**

In this exercise, you'll work at keeping close possession of the ball, dribbling it around the opposition in a tight loop and making sure to block them out of the play.

On the pitch below is a hypothetical player formation, where your players are in green and the opposition are in yellow. Dribble the ball in a single loop around the pitch by connecting some cones, so that each number is surrounded by the specified number of adjacent line segments. Cones can only be joined by horizontal or vertical lines. The loop cannot touch, cross or overlap itself in any way.

When your loop is complete, all players in your team must be inside the loop, and all opposition players must be outside it.

⏱ **Can you block off the opposition and complete your loop in less than five minutes? If you do, you've scored a penalty. If you take more than ten minutes, you're booked!**

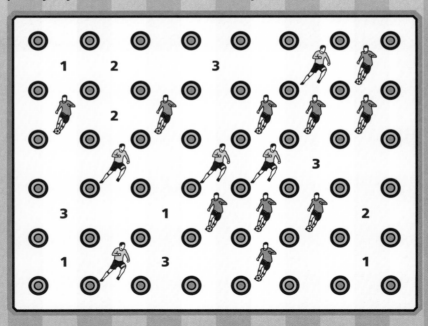

# UP FRONT

**In the tactics room, the manager has some issues to iron out before your final match of the group stage.**

The coach wants to instil some confidence in the strikers, mindful that courage and composure will be the keys to them breaking through the opposition's defence. The idea is to demonstrate how they can calculate their best running lines and make an informed decision about when to try to get behind the defence.

On the pitch below, your team's forwards are marked with numbers. Can you map out the squares they can cover in each direction by drawing one or more horizontal or vertical lines leading away from each player? The numbers tell you how many squares the lines from each player cover, not including the numbered square itself. Each empty square on the pitch must be reached by one of the players' lines, but no more than one player's line can enter any square. All the lines from one of the players have been drawn in to show how it works.

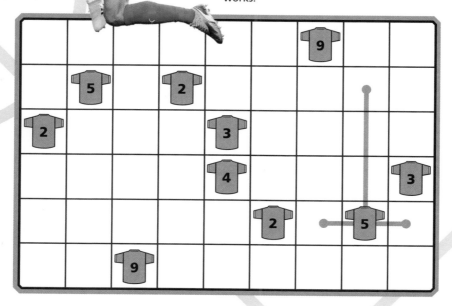

SOLUTION ON PAGE **194**

# INTERCEPTION

**With the team feeling a little more confident after a few days' training, your manager has one last scenario to run through before the big game tomorrow.**

The biggest weakness in the previous match was an inability to stop the opposition's momentum when they were heading towards your goal – which, unfortunately, happened a lot. This tactics session looks closely at anticipating the paths of opposing players to intercept the ball.

On the map below, the beginning and end points of a run made by the opposition have been marked, starting at one yellow player and ending at the other. The green dots on the field are points that they can take the ball to on their run, and your job is to work out where they'll travel. Draw a path that joins one yellow player to the other via the green dots, using only horizontal and vertical lines. The path cannot cross any shaded squares (representing your team's players), and no dot can be used more than once. Numbers outside the grid reveal the total number of dots visited by the path in their corresponding row or column.

There are three points at which you could intercept the opposition's run, which are marked A, B and C. Which one of the points is on the completed path, revealing where a player from your team could make an interception?

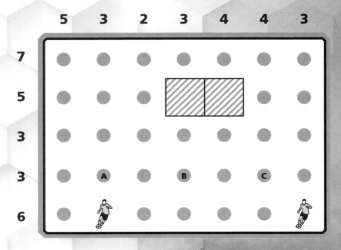

# CLOSE ATTENTION

In the FIFA World Cup™ – even in the group stage – you can't leave anything to chance. You and the team have been training hard on set pieces to give yourselves the best shot at winning, and it looks like you're ready to put your previous loss behind you and move on to the next round. As always, your manager thinks there's still work to be done, however, and wants to quickly fit in another session before game time.

In particular, the team's approach to defending free kicks is under the microscope. Although it's important for the team to trust their instincts, the coaching staff want everyone to really watch the ball – and the other players – to stop them making any impulsive moves that might jeopardise the defence. Instead of lining everyone up on the training pitch, however, they've devised a quick visual exercise to see how well you do at anticipating the motion of the ball.

On the image of the free kick opposite, there's one important thing missing: the ball. Work out which square in the grid you think the ball should be in, and then make a note of that square's coordinates. Once you're done, see how well you did by comparing your choice against the scoreboard below, depending on how close you were to the answer given in the solutions. Trace a path from your solution to the ball's real position, first with a horizontal line and then a vertical one. Then count how many squares – if any – are between your solution and the correct one.

## How did you score?

| 4+ squares away: Another booking! | 3 squares away: Sloppy spectator | 2 squares away: Average observer | 1 square away: Eagle-eyed | Right on target: Penalty scored! |
|---|---|---|---|---|

your answer in the grid below.

# FREE KICK

**It's the final match of the group stage, and you're in the tunnel ready to get out on to the pitch. If you win this game, you'll come second in the group and go through to the knockout rounds. On the other hand, a loss or a draw means that you'll be out, so it is basically a knockout tie already!**

In the first few minutes, your players are looking calm and composed – it's the complete opposite of the previous match. You think they can put all their hard work into practice and get the win they deserve.

On the 30-minute mark, your team are awarded a free kick after a foul by the opposition. Now is the time for smart calculation and decisive action if you want to turn this chance into a goal. On the map of the penalty area on the opposite page, can you work out the best place to aim the ball, based on who is visible from the kicker's position?

Place 1 to 5 once each into every row and column of the box, with each digit representing a player. Place digits in the grid in such a way that each given clue number outside the grid shows the number of players that are "visible"

from that point, looking along that clue's row or column. A player is visible unless preceded by a player represented by a higher digit, reading in order along that row or column. For example, in 21435, the 2, 4 and 5 are visible from the left, but the 1 is obscured by the 2, and the 3 by the 4, so the clue for this would be 3.

When you've finished, you need to be able to play the free kick straight to a player numbered 4, as you know that's your best chance of scoring. Which of the three arrows shows a direction where 4 is visible from that point?

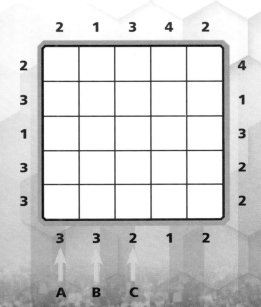

SOLUTION ON PAGE 195

# SHOTS ON TARGET

**Good news! You're a goal up going into the second half, and you're hoping to gain some breathing space by extending your lead.**

It's a good job you and the team practised heading, as there are plenty of set pieces in the second half that can be turned into further goalscoring opportunities. Below is a map of the pitch, showing the efforts on target by each team in the second half. Can you work out the path of each shot, and reveal which of them were goals?

Some of the shots were deflected. The start and end points of each of these are marked with identical balls: yellow balls show opposition shots, while green ones are from your team. Draw diagonal lines across certain squares to represent players, with exactly one player per bold-lined region, except for one containing a square that holds a player from both teams. The players must be placed so that a ball travelling vertically into the

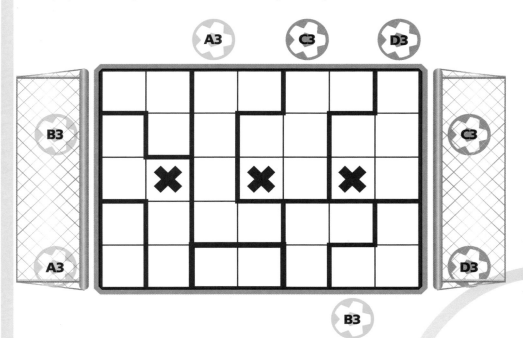

grid from each lettered clue above or below the grid would then exit the grid at the same letter horizontally on either goal line, having been deflected by the exact number of players indicated by the number next to the letter. Deflections always result in a 90-degree turn – you can check back to your heading training session for more details if necessary.

Once you've placed the players, take a look at the path of each shot. All of them reach one of the goal lines at either end, but those that travel through a square marked with an "X" en route were saved. Given that paths between green balls are shots by your team, while paths between yellow balls are the opposition's, how many of each team's shots were successful?

# ROUND OF 16

Congratulations! You've made it out of the group stage and you're through to the last 16, but you only came second in your group, so the entire squad know that you will have to up your game to continue to progress. You will be facing even better teams from now on.

Every match counts now that you are into the knockout stage. In this round, there's just one match to play, so you'll spend more time focusing on your skills in training and honing your matchday tactics to get you ready for the big game.

To stay in the competition, you'll need to show consistency in order to win every match from this point on.

**So let's get training!**

# WARM-UP

**Let's kick off your preparations for this round of the tournament with a familiar warm-up exercise.**

The squad are all feeling pretty stiff after three games on the bounce, so the coaching team want to ease you back into training. Dribble the ball in a loop around the obstacles on the pitch, starting and ending with the player placed in the grid. Make sure to visit every empty square, but without visiting any square more than once. Diagonal moves between squares aren't allowed, and you must avoid entering any square containing a training cone.

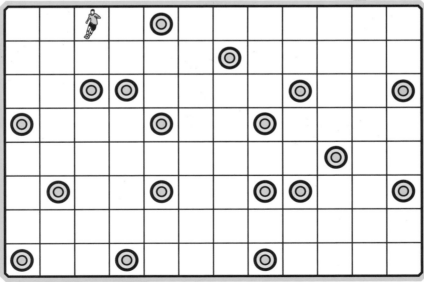

# THROUGH-BALL

**Now that you're warmed up, it's time to practise your footballing skills. Let's start with passing into space.**

To give yourself the best chance in the rest of the tournament, you'll need to stay one step ahead of your opponents – literally. It's important that you anticipate not just the opposition's movements, but also the runs that your team-mates make. This allows you to pass into the area ahead of them, getting in behind the defence, and fully utilising the pace of your star strikers. Ideally, when they make their move, they will free themselves from the last defenders, and then it's up to you to find them with a pinpoint through-ball.

In this exercise, you'll test your ability to analyse the current state of play by looking at the training grid below. Each of the footballs has just been passed into an empty space, and needs a player to run on to it to be able to play on. Associate each player with exactly one football, using either a horizontal or vertical line to join them together. Lines cannot cross over each other, nor over another ball or player.

⏱ **Can you complete the exercise in less than four minutes? If you do, congratulations! You have successfully scored a penalty. If you take more than eight minutes, then unfortunately you have been booked and must turn to the Referee's Table on page 222.**

SOLUTION ON PAGE **197**

# DARE TO DREAM?

**In your next match, you'll be playing the winner of one of the other groups, so you know you'll be facing a confident team.**

This particular nation are famously unpredictable in their tactics, so you'll need to stay alert during the match. Even for your world-class management team, it's almost impossible to predict their game plan, so the boss has put faith in you to track it as the match is in play. It's essential that you have the ability to look up, quickly take in your surroundings, and adapt your own play as needed.

Practise your visual perception skills with the celebratory team photos opposite. There are a lot of distractions – more than normal on a football pitch – but it is important to be prepared for anything, even ticker tape. The photos are similar, but not identical. Can you spot the ten differences between the two images?

Time how long it takes you to find the first five differences before continuing, and compare your time to the scoreboard below.

| How did you score? | | | | |
|---|---|---|---|---|
| ⏱ More than 5 minutes: You've been booked! | ⏱ 4-5 minutes: Slow spectator | ⏱ 3-4 minutes: Average observer | ⏱ 2-3 minutes: Eagle-eyed | ⏱ Less than 2 minutes: Penalty scored! |

SOLUTION ON PAGE 197

# BALANCED PLAY

**After your first training sessions since reaching the knockout stage, it's time to have a think about some tactics. Never forget that mental agility will get you a long way on the football field, given you already have the world-class skills needed for success.**

Your manager wants to test the team's reaction skills, to see how you respond in real time to the changing dynamics of the match. It's crucial for players to be spread evenly around the pitch, so that no areas are left undefended or become too far to get to if the play opens up. The team also need to be able to react quickly and correct their positioning if part of the playing area is becoming needlessly busy.

Build your skills by balancing the field opposite to make sure that neither your players, nor the opposition players, are dominating any part of the pitch. Your team are wearing green, while the opposition are in yellow. Insert players of both teams into the grid, but to avoid overcrowding, ensure that no lines of four or more players from the same team are formed in any direction, including diagonally.

Before you begin, start your stopwatch. When you're done, stop the clock and compare your time against the scoreboard opposite.

SOLUTION ON PAGE 197

## How did you score?

| ⏱ More than 7 minutes: You're booked! | ⏱ 5-7 minutes: Average performer | ⏱ 3-5 minutes: Fair play | ⏱ 2-3 minutes: Star scorer | ⏱ Less than 2 minutes: Penalty scored! |

# MAN-MARKING

**Your coach is fast becoming a big fan of man-marking and wants to make sure the team are up to scratch on it and fully ready for the first knockout match. To guarantee that all the bases are covered, each player in the team is being assigned to mark a player on the opposing side, so that no gaps can open up in the defence. It's exhausting work, but it has worked well in the past.**

Practise your man-marking on the pitch below by assigning exactly one defender to mark each attacker, shown in yellow. The defenders must be immediately next to the attacking players, in a touching square in one of the four main directions.

You must also make sure that every row and column contains the number of defenders given at the end of the row or column in question.

To keep the formation balanced, defenders cannot be in touching squares – not even diagonally.

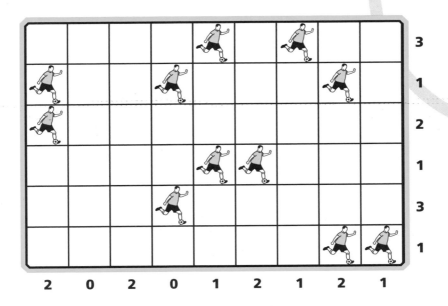

# FIND THE DEFENDERS

**You're back on the pitch for more training and, as promised, it's time to up your game. The next exercise builds on skills you've been practising in the first rounds of the competition, while asking you to think outside the proverbial box a little bit more.**

In the training exercise below, you aren't given marked cones to look out for. Instead, it's up to you to anticipate where defenders will appear on the pitch. You'll need to pay attention to the extra information around you and react accordingly.

Dribble the ball in a loop around the pitch, while detecting and avoiding defenders. The loop cannot re-enter any square, and any empty squares that the loop does not visit must be shaded – this is where the defenders are located. Shaded squares cannot touch, except diagonally – the opposing team have practised balancing their play! Arrows in some squares show the exact number of opposition defenders (i.e. shaded squares) in a given direction in their row or column. Not all shaded squares are necessarily identified with arrows – so keep your eyes peeled for hidden defenders as you create your loop.

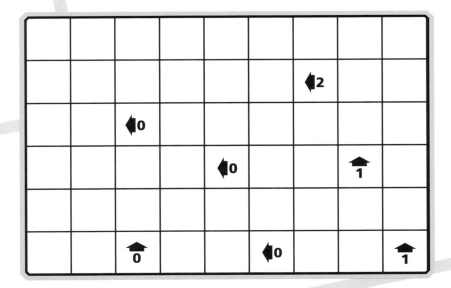

# MATCHING PAIRS

**Discipline is key to a smooth performance on the pitch, and your manager has impeccable standards.**

The team are also expected to maintain a high level of orderliness off the pitch – and that means keeping the dressing room organised. Unfortunately, after celebrating your advance into the knockout stage, not everything is where it should be, and the boss isn't happy. Plus, it's pretty difficult to show off your skills on the world stage wearing two left-footed shoes!

You need to sort out the tangle of boots below. Can you match up five identical pairs of boots and identify the one that doesn't have a pair?

SOLUTION ON PAGE **198**

# ZONE DEFENCE

**In an earlier tactics session, you mapped out some initial man-marking for the next match.**

You and your team-mates have all been assigned players to mark for the match, and you'll need to be on their tail whenever they have the ball. However, the manager wants the team to be able to adapt to the opposition's unpredictable tactics, and so has decided that you should practise some zone-defence skills as well, in case there is the need for a quick change of system.

The coaching staff have devised a map of the midfield – shown below – indicating the areas that the individual players in the opposing team (excluding the goalkeeper and two central defenders) usually cover. Can you work out where you and your team-mates will need to focus your efforts in midfield, so that you can mark your players but keep the play open?

Place players in some squares so that each row, column and outlined region contains exactly two players. To make sure the play is balanced, players cannot touch each other – not even diagonally.

# ONE TOUCH

**Your team got through the group stage by making sure your passing game was clinical – that is, that almost nothing was intercepted by the opposing team.**

Your team need to be able to move quickly and assuredly once you're in possession of the ball, and your manager wants to make sure that your accuracy doesn't slip. That's the thinking behind the training exercise below, where the numbers on the pitch sketch out exactly the number of touches needed to score a goal. How quickly can you score in 34 touches?

Pass the ball around the pitch by writing a number in every empty square, so each number from 1 to 34 appears once in the grid. Numbers must be placed so as to form a path from 1 to the goal, moving in any direction at each step to a touching square one higher in value – or from square 34 to the goal. Diagonal steps are allowed.

Before you start placing numbers and making your path, set a timer. When you're done, stop the clock and compare your time against the scoreboard below.

| 23 |    |    |    |    | ⚽1 |    |
|----|----|----|----|----|----|----|
|    | 24 | 🥅 |    | 11 |    |    |
| 25 |    |    |    | 12 |    | 4  |
|    |    |    |    | 13 | 8  |    |
| 28 |    |    | 15 |    |    | 6  |

### How did you score?

| ⏱ More than 7 minutes: Too slow. You're booked! | ⏱ 5-7 minutes: Fair effort | ⏱ 3-5 minutes: Star scorer | ⏱ Less than 3 minutes: Penalty scored! |

SOLUTION ON PAGE 199

# FORMATION

**It's almost game time, and your manager needs to decide on the starting formation. Shown on the right is an initial configuration for how the ten outfield players need to be grouped together in sets on the field.**

There are six separate "sets" of players shown in the image above: one set of three adjacent players; two sets of two adjacent players; and then three players placed on their own. Can you work out where your manager plans to place them, according to the clues you can see on the half-complete tactics board below?

Place the given sets of players – in the quantities and set formations shown – into the grid, placing each set of two or more either horizontally or vertically. Different player sets cannot be in touching squares – not even diagonally. Squares where players will be needed are indicated by the numbers outside the grid, which show the exact number of squares in their row or column that must be occupied by players. No more than one player can be placed in a single square.

Complete the board to discover the final formation your manager has in mind for the match. Three have been placed into the grid already, to get you started.

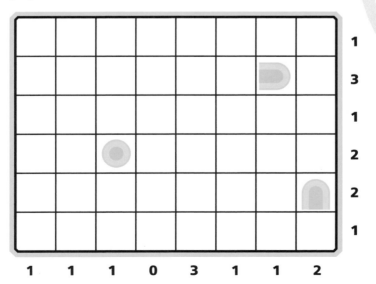

# CROWDED BOX

...r next match is a must-win, so it's crucial that your focus doesn't ...at any point during those 90 minutes. In most of your tactics ...ons, you've looked at how your team's players need to spread ...mselves out evenly to cover everyone. But what about when ...need to group together?

...oaching staff want to see how you respond to high-pressure situations when ...'s a lot of activity around you – it's vital that you stay calm and don't take your ...ff the ball, either literally or figuratively. When things get busy inside your ...box you need to make sure you're ready to respond quickly to the accelerating ...making the right calls so that your team can stay ahead in the game. They ...to know that you can rapidly scan the scene and react to what you see. ...he photo of the crowded box below, the ball has been removed. Can you ...out which grid square the ball should be located in, based on the eyelines and ...ons of the players shown?

...your answer in the grid below, as in previous questions of this type ...age 70). If you get it exactly right, you have scored a penalty. If you ...ore than four squares away, you are booked and must turn to the ...ee's Table on page 222.

# MORE CROSS-FIELD FUN

**Cross-field passing is a nifty technique that you practised in the qualifiers, and the coaching staff think it's high time for a refresher course.**

Aerial passes are quite evidently harder for the opposition to intercept – but it's also harder for your team-mates to get on the end of them. Each player on the training field has been assigned a partner, whom they need to pass the ball to by sending it over the heads of other nearby players, making sure it doesn't touch the ground before it reaches their partner.

Can you map out all of the cross-field passes on the training pitch? Join each pair of identically numbered players by drawing a path from one to the other. These paths can travel horizontally, vertically or diagonally between squares. No more than one path can enter any square, but paths *can* cross if they do so diagonally on the join between four squares.

⏱ **When switching play with a cross-field pass, timing is key. If you take too long on the ball, the opposition gain extra time to get into position and try to intercept it. Can you complete all of the passes in under four minutes? If you do, congratulations! You have scored a penalty.**

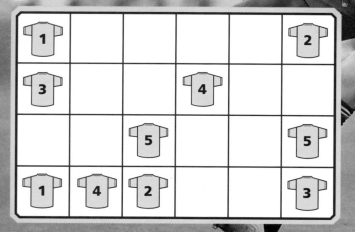

# THE POINT OF NO RETURN

**On the tactics board, your manager unpacks a scenario that's been on display in recent matches, which the staff aren't happy about.**

They've noticed that, when making a run with the ball, some players fail to anticipate their path fully and get themselves into a position that's impossible to score from, or even pass the ball. They want players to think much further in advance to avoid creating a sticky situation that they cannot later get out of.

On the board, they've sketched out some zones that a player could try to break into with the ball if they gain possession. Now use them to draw a loop that visits every square, travelling only horizontally or vertically between squares, and without visiting any square more than once. The loop can only enter and exit every bold-lined region once each – this is because it's important for every route to have an exit strategy, since you cannot go back on yourself once you've entered a zone.

Shown on the board are four sets of arrows, indicating possible places where a player might choose to enter some zones. Two of them are incorrect, however, and would lead to an incomplete loop if a player were to plan a route that included these crossover points. Once you've mapped out your complete loop according to the instructions from your manager, can you identify which two sets of arrows are not correct and would leave a player in trouble further down the line if the route had followed them?

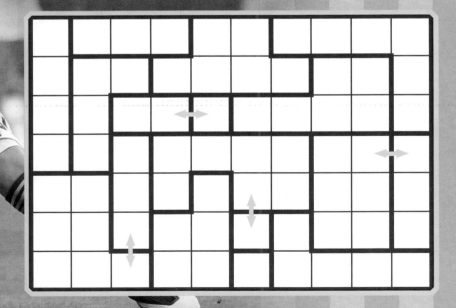

SOLUTION ON PAGE 200

# GOAL OR SAVE?

**Before the big game, your team have to practise one more scenario – penalties.**

Now that you're in the knockout stage, extra time and penalties have both been introduced to make sure there's a clear winner at the end. You need all of your team-mates – not just the goalkeeper – to be able to pick up on small visual clues, which will help them to anticipate the opposition's actions, whether it's the keeper or the penalty-taker. Are your team ready for the one-on-one challenge?

Take a look at the four images of penalties on these two pages. In each of them, the ball has been removed from the image but everything else remains the same. Can you say, for each image, which penalties went in and which were saved?

# GET INTO SPACE

**It's game time! After plenty of training sessions, and thorough tactical analysis, your team are ready for their game in the round of 16.**

The tension is high. This is a must-win, and as you lead your team out down the tunnel and on to the pitch, you try your best to keep your composure.

Finally, the whistle is blown and the match begins! At last, it's time to put your training into action – specifically your through-balls. You are in possession of the ball and need to pass it into an empty space so a team-mate can run on to it. On the pitch below, can you map out which spaces you could pass the ball into in order to give your team-mates the best chance of reaching it?

Place balls into some empty squares in the grid. Each number represents a player, and the value of each number tells you the number of touching squares that can have a ball passed into them – including diagonally. No more than one ball may be placed per square, and nor can they be placed in squares that contain players.

Can you work out where all the balls can be placed, based on each player's position?

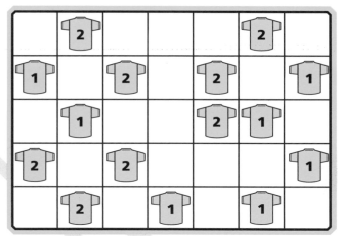

# ZONES OF CONTROL

IIt's half-time and at the moment, the match is goalless. Your manager wants to work out the areas in which your team are dominating the field in order to see where the majority of your possession is and build on the strengths of the first half.

Can you create a possession map of the pitch below, showing the areas of the pitch in which each player – represented by a number – has had most control of the ball?

Draw along some of the dashed grid lines to divide the pitch into a set of non-overlapping rectangles and/or squares, so that each shape contains one number and every number is contained within one shape. The number in each shape must be exactly equal to the number of squares contained in that shape.

⏱ **You only have a few minutes before you have to go back out on to the pitch. If you can complete it successfully in less than five minutes, you score a penalty. If it takes you more than ten minutes, then take a card from the Referee's Table on page 222.**

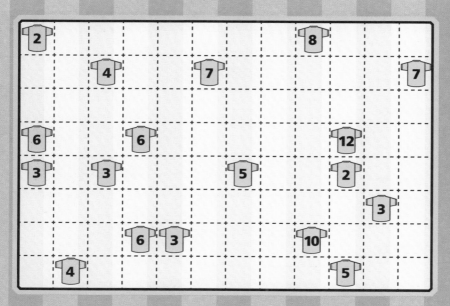

SOLUTION ON PAGE **202**

# LINES OF CERTAINTY

**It's crunch time. The game is in the 60<sup>th</sup> minute, but there are still no goals from either team. You have just been awarded a free kick, but although you're tempted, it's not quite the right angle to take a shot at goal yourself.**

You need to cross it to one of your own players waiting inside the box for your delivery. Can you use the stats below to create a map of where you should kick the ball, based on who is visible in the penalty box?

Place 1 to 5 once each into every row and column of the grid. Place digits in the grid in such a way that each given clue number outside the grid represents the number of digits that are "visible" from that point, looking along that clue's row or column. A digit is visible unless there is a higher digit preceding it, reading in order along that row or column. For example, in 21435, the 2, 4 and 5 are visible from the left, but the 1 is obscured by the 2, and the 3 by the 4, giving a clue of 3 when viewed from the left.

When you've finished, you need to be able to play the free kick to a player numbered 1, as you know that's your best chance of scoring. Which of the three arrows shows a direction where 1 is visible from the position of the kick?

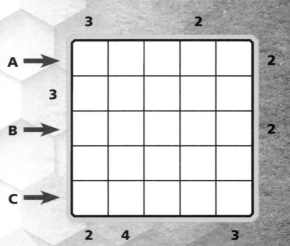

# UNDER PRESSURE

**Your team manage to score a goal from the free kick, but the opposition respond swiftly. Suddenly, you find yourself back to level pegging, at 1-1. You need to score another goal or it's extra time – unless they score first, in which case it's time to check out of the team hotel.**

The manager shouts at you from the touchline to utilise the precision passing that got you through the group stage. Can you work out a technique on the pitch opposite that allows you to score at least two more goals, with only a restricted number of passes available?

Each of the numbered shirts represents a player in position. Join numbers with horizontal or vertical lines, with each line representing the ball being passed once between players. All of the players must have as many lines connected to them as specified by the value on their shirt. No more than two passes may join any pair of players, and no passes may cross. The finished layout must connect all players, so the ball can travel from any player to any other by following one or more of the pass lines. Any lines that pass through stars are goals scored for your team, while stars that aren't visited represent goals for the opposition.

When you've completed the puzzle, the whistle blows. Look at the pitch. Who scored each of the three goals, and what was the final score in the match?

# QUARTER-FINALS

You've successfully navigated your way through your first knockout match after a dramatic second-half performance. Following a nervy and goalless first half, you managed to pull it together and use precision passing to get your team into the right goalscoring positions. Just like you'd practised in training!

There are now just eight teams left in the competition, and none of your competitors are showing any sign of running out of steam. To beat the next team you'll face, your players will need to be at their fittest – and their minds at their sharpest.

There's some fine-tuning to do before the quarter-final, so, in the next training and tactics sessions, you'll work on some problem areas, as well as on perfecting the basics. When the big game arrives, will you have what it takes to lead your team through to the semis?

**There's only one place to start, so it's time to head back over to the training pitch.**

# WARM-UP

**Your manager is keen to ensure that you don't lose your winning momentum.**

With that in mind, a speed fitness test has been set for the team, involving a lot of cones. Every player in the squad will take the test and you're up first. How fast can you create a loop that visits every cone on the pitch once each?

Map out a running circuit that visits all of the cones on the pitch below, forming a single loop. The circuit cannot cross or touch itself at any point and, to avoid confusion, no diagonal moves between cones are allowed. Some parts of the circuit have already been marked in.

Before you start mapping out your running loop, start your stopwatch. When you're done, stop the clock and compare your time against the scoreboard below.

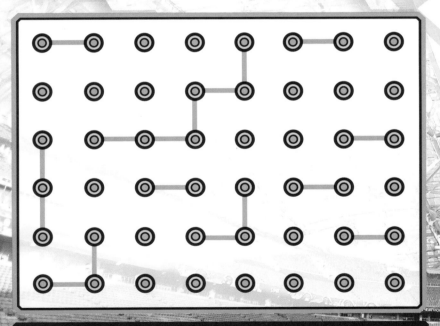

## How did you score?

| ⏱ More than 6 minutes: You're booked! | ⏱ 5-6 minutes: Average performer | ⏱ 4-5 minutes: Fair game | ⏱ 3-4 minutes: Star scorer | ⏱ Less than 3 minutes: Penalty scored! |

# TOTAL FOOTBALL

**Now that you're deeper into the knockout stage, the competition has really ramped up. The next side you'll be facing are famed for their tactical flexibility, and their manager is a big believer in a "total football" approach – meaning that the opposing team will be ready for anything you throw at them, figuratively or otherwise.**

Instead of using strict man-marking, the opposition players are trained in all positions, so that if gaps open up on the pitch, any player can fill them. Your manager has a plan, though.

Given how quickly the other team can flip from defence to attack, and between defensive systems, your manager wants you and your team-mates to be able to anticipate how much space the opposing players can use to their advantage. The coaching staff have mapped out a hypothetical playing situation on the pitch below and want you to work out how much ground a player can cover in either direction.

Draw along some of the grid lines to divide the grid into a set of regions. Every region must contain exactly one player, and the region must be symmetrical in such a way that, if rotated 180 degrees around the player, it would look exactly the same. The regions can be any shape (not just square or rectangular), so long as they are symmetrical, and every part of the field must be covered by one region. One region is marked in already as an example.

# CLOSE ANALYSIS

The boss has asked you to help out with some opposition scouting. Knowing their star player's feints and tricks inside out could be the difference between successfully winning possession or being embarrassingly nutmegged. Take a close look at the original image, and then the four images labelled A-D. Only one is an exact mirror image. How quickly can you identify the correct one?

**How did you score?**

| ⏱ More than 7 minutes: You're booked! | ⏱ 5-7 minutes: Slow spectator | ⏱ 3-5 minutes: Average observer | ⏱ 2-3 minutes: Eagle-eyed | ⏱ Less than 2 minutes: Penalty scored! |
|---|---|---|---|---|

SOLUTION ON PAGE **204**

# DEFENSIVE ZONES

The coaching staff are concerned that the team's reaction speeds are not up to scratch, especially when turning attack into defence. They want to know that you can make this physical and mental shift quickly and accurately. You'll need to expect the unexpected – and be able to deal with it – to stay on top of the game.

They draw up some hypothetical defensive zones on the tactics board, which are shown below.

The manager asks how many defensive zones there are. At first glance, you think that there appear to be five main zones, but your boss isn't happy with that response. Look again!

How many rectangular zones, outlined in black, can you count in total on the pitch? There are more rectangles than you might think, including the big one all around the outside of the pitch. Once you think you've found them all, take a look at the manager's solution to see if you missed any, then compare your performance against the scorecard on the right.

**How many did you miss?**

**10 or more:** Booked!

**7-9:** Foul

**5-6:** Getting there

**3-4:** On target

**1-2:** Well tackled

**None:** Penalty scored!

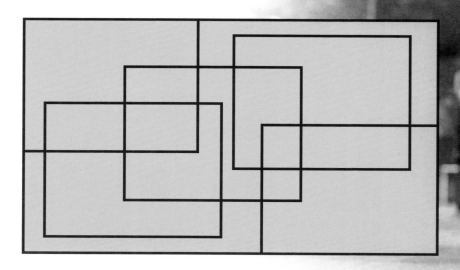

# CONE CHALLENGE

**It's time to get back on the pitch for some more training. You're confident that the team are passing quickly and accurately, and the round-of-16 result is strong evidence of that. But what about good, old-fashioned dribbling to get through the defence?**

Your upcoming opposition are great at turning defence into attack, and ball-control skills will be crucial against a team who are sure to be hyper-aggressive in their marking. Maintaining possession and limiting any opportunities for them to counter-attack will need to be mastered before your next match, which means keeping the ball close to you. Can you control the ball around the pitch below, following the rules determined by the different cones?

Dribble the ball in a single loop that passes over the centre of every cone on the pitch, using only horizontal and vertical lines. The loop must pass in a straight line over every blue cone, then make a 90-degree turn in one or both of the preceding and following squares. Conversely, the loop must make a 90-degree turn at every orange cone, but travel straight through both the preceding and following squares without turning. The loop cannot visit any square more than once but does not need to visit every square.

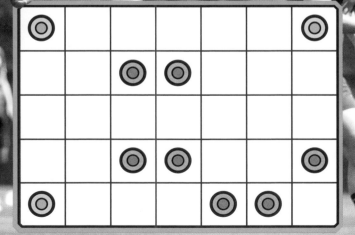

SOLUTION ON PAGE **204**

# ASSEMBLE YOUR TEAM

Team cohesion is absolutely key at any time, but during knockout football, it is tested like on no other occasion. Mistakes are bound to happen, but it is the way your team rebound from them that will determine if you are to become just another also-ran, or take your place among the greats as a World Cup-winning team.

The boss wants to ensure that morale is as high as possible, and that you know your team inside out. The photographer has been taking some snaps during training and the manager has cut one up into 15 pieces.
   You have now been tasked with a very literal team-building exercise. Can you rebuild the original image successfully? Ideally, everyone in the squad should be instantly recognisable to you, from their shoes to their hairstyles, so you have been given a time limit for your task. Time yourself, and after you have finished, check how you have done against the scoreboard below.

## How did you score?

| ⏱ More than 7 minutes: Card conceded! | ⏱ 5-7 minutes: Slow spectator | ⏱ 4-5 minutes: Average observer | ⏱ 3-4 minutes: Eagle-eyed | ⏱ Less than 3 minutes: Penalty scored! |

SOLUTION ON PAGE **205**

# PARSING FITNESS

**Satisfied that your mental fitness has been sufficiently primed, the boss wants to look at physical agility next.**

Throughout the tournament, your team have been using wearable technology, which logs data for each player. Your manager wants you to analyse this. The pitch below has been partly completed with some of the data from the last match.

To fill in the rest, place a number in every empty square so that each number in the grid forms part of a continuous playing area of that many squares, so for example a 4 is in a playing area of exactly four squares. Playing areas of the same size cannot touch, except diagonally. You can draw along the dashed lines to keep track of completed playing areas. One area is marked in already, as an example.

Each area, when complete, represents a zone covered by one player in the match. The higher the numbers, the fitter the players, so the further they'll be able to run. Once the grid is completed, take a look at the results. How many player zones on the pitch show a fitness score of 4?

|   | 2 | 5 | 5 | 5 | 5 |   |
|---|---|---|---|---|---|---|
| 1 | 4 | 5 | 1 |   |   | 9 |
|   | 4 |   | 3 |   | 9 |   |
|   | 4 |   | 6 | 9 |   |   |
| 1 |   | 1 | 5 | 9 |   | 2 |
|   | 2 | 6 |   | 4 |   |   |

# CENTRAL STRENGTH

**Despite being pleased with the starting formation from the most recent match, your manager is thinking of going with a midfield four this time round, rather than the usual three.**

It's a tactical change that comes with risks, given that the old formation has worked well for the team so far. The coaching staff are sure, however, that it will prove to be a helpful set-up against the next opposition; more bodies in the centre of the pitch might help to defend against their more flexible style of play.

Your manager has mapped out the midfield below and wants to make sure that all four midfielders will be able to cover and defend an equal amount of the pitch; otherwise, the change might introduce gaps, which the opposition could take advantage of. Can you help to work out a way in which the whole midfield can be covered equally by the four players?

Draw along some of the dashed grid lines on the pitch in order to divide this midfield into four regions – one for each player. The regions must all be identical in size and shape, although they may be rotated (but not reflected) relative to one another.

SOLUTION ON PAGE **205**

# BEAUTIFUL *TIKI-TAKA*

## The coaching team now want you to focus on quick passing.

You're confident that the dribbling exercises earlier have reinforced the basics for the team, and your through-passing – which proved so crucial in the round of 16 – is in great shape. Now is a good time, therefore, to practise short passes and, in particular, the *tiki-taka* style in which your team can use lots of quick, short passing movements to get themselves into great attacking positions.

Below is a map of the training pitch, with training cones once again set out. The manager wants you to create a looping route by passing the ball from cone to cone.

Draw lines connecting some pairs of cones, with each line between cones representing a single short pass. All the lines must form a single loop, with no crossings or leftover parts, so that each digit has the specified number of adjacent line segments. Cones can only be joined by horizontal or vertical lines. A "0" means that the loop must not pass by that number.

⏱ **Speed is the name of the game, so time yourself. If you completed the exercise in fewer than five minutes, you scored a penalty! If it took you more than ten minutes, then turn to the Referee's Table on page 222.**

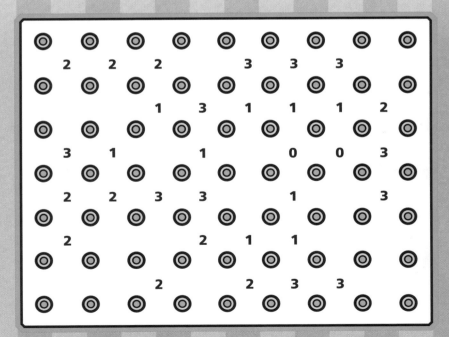

# BALANCE THE PLAY

**Previously, the manager tested the team's reaction speed to make sure that they could quickly look up and help balance out the pitch.**

Your team did well in training but, under the pressure of the knockout stage and the noise from the crowd, some of the team struggled to implement their skills.

Your manager is keen to make sure that all of the players stay focused and keep an eye on the big picture. To this end, can you balance the midfield below to make sure that neither your team, nor the opposition, overcrowd any area?

Every orange player on the pitch represents a player from your team, and a blue player is an opposition player. Fill the rest of the midfield by placing a blue or orange player into every empty square, so that there are an equal number of players from each team within every row and every column. To make sure there's no overcrowding, there must be no more than two players of the same team in succession when reading along any row or column.

⏱ **Quick scanning is important, so time yourself. If you completed the exercise in fewer than six minutes, you scored a penalty! If it took you more than 12 minutes, then turn to the Referee's Table on page 222.**

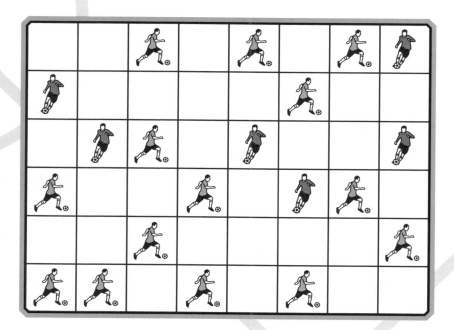

SOLUTION ON PAGE 206

# A NEW FORMATION

After the earlier tactics session, your manager has decided to go ahead and use four players in midfield, hoping this will limit the opposition's ability to break through and make their way up the pitch. Essentially, the idea is to block off the middle of the pitch so that, even if they do get the ball, they have fewer areas to which they can travel with it.

The team need to be able to visualise not only where the opposition players will attack, but what spaces could be open to them around the pitch when they counter. To help with this, the manager has come up with a plan that means that each opposition player can be blocked into a certain area on the pitch, with only a small amount of wiggle room each way. Can you prove that you and the team can execute the plan?

On the pitch on the opposite page are numbered shirts, where each number represents one of the opposition players. Draw along the grid lines so that each player is contained within either a 1x2 or 1x3 rectangular block, placed either horizontally or vertically. The secret, however, is to place these blocks in order to limit the movement of the players, so that the blocks can only immediately "slide" into the number of empty spaces indicated by the number within that block. Horizontal blocks only slide horizontally, and vertical blocks only slide vertically.

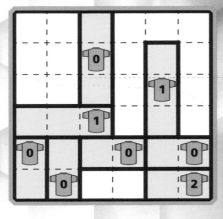

Take a look at the example on the left to see how this works. The 0-blocks can't immediately slide into any squares since they are fully blocked, while the horizontal and vertical 1-blocks can each slide into just one square. The 2-block can slide into two squares.

# SPEED SKILLS

**The big game is tomorrow! Your manager is pleased with the tactical work you've done, and the team are expecting a challenge – but they're pretty much ready.**

Take a look at the scenario below. The two orange shirts represent players in your team. You're on the left with the ball, and your star striker is on the right. The two blue players are defenders from the opposition, and they're making your life difficult. If you pass now, even if your striker scores, the goal will be disallowed for offside. But if your forward moves to the left before you pass, there's a high chance the ball will be intercepted by one of the defenders. Can you instead mark out a path where you can dribble the ball from the position you're in now to the striker's position?

Join some of the dots with horizontal and vertical lines to make a single path from you to your team-mate, which does not revisit any dot. Numbers outside the pitch reveal the exact number of dots in their row or column that must be visited by the path, including the start and end dots. You can visit any number of dots in unlabelled rows and columns. The path can't touch or cross any of the defender boxes, since you don't want to give them the opportunity to gain possession of the ball.

1

6

5

3

5

# IN AND OUT

**It's the final training session before the quarter-final tomorrow and you're feeling ready to take on the opposition. Your manager has put you all through your paces, and the mental work you've been doing on tactical analysis puts you in a great position to anticipate the other team's movements. The coaching team have devised a final task to help make sure you're mentally and physically ready for tomorrow's challenge.**

Your objective in this training exercise is to create a loop around the pitch using a series of short passes, to help block off the opposition and keep you away from defenders in the centre. Luckily, you'll be able to draw on many of the techniques you've been working on since your last knockout match.

Draw a single loop on the pitch by connecting some cones, so that each number is adjacent to that many line segments. Diagonal connections aren't allowed, and the loop cannot cross itself or revisit a cone. The loop must be designed so that you (indicated by the orange player) are inside the loop, and both the opposition players (shown in blue) are outside it.

Have you got what it takes? It's time to put your training so far into action!

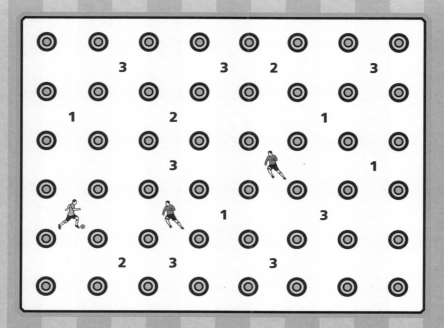

SOLUTION ON PAGE **207**

# READING THE GAME

**With less than 24 hours before kick-off, the manager wants you and the team to save your legs. However, it's important that you stay as mentally alert as ever, and so the boss has devised an exercise for you to take part in.**

The previous match had a chaotic second half and knockout football has a habit of creating excitingly frenetic finishes. With any luck, you will be far enough ahead that you can close out the game in a calm fashion, but you have to be prepared for anything. The manager has chosen an image for you to examine that contains a lot of action, with players jumping, heading and punching at the ball in the box. However, the ball has been removed from the image entirely.

Can you work out, from the positions and eyelines of the players shown, where the ball would be at the moment when the photo was taken? Work out which square in the grid you think the ball should be in, and then make a note of that square's coordinates. Once you're done, see how well you did by comparing your choice against the scoreboard below. Trace a path from your square to the ball's real position, first with a horizontal line and then a vertical one. Then count how many squares – if any – are between your solution and the correct one.

## How did you score?

| 4+ squares away: Another booking! | 3 squares away: Sloppy spectator | 2 squares away: Average observer | 1 square away: Eagle-eyed | Right on target: Penalty scored! |

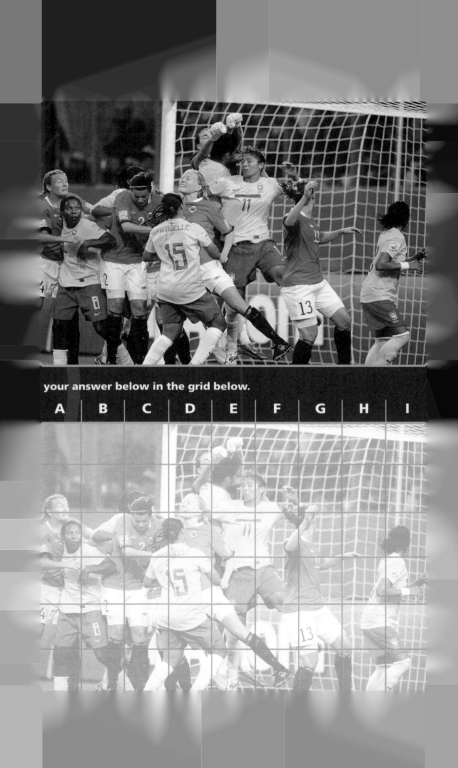

your answer below in the grid below.

| A | B | C | D | E | F | G | H | I |
|---|---|---|---|---|---|---|---|---|

# LOOKING IN

It's game time! You're feeling surprisingly calm – both prepared and ready – when the whistle blows and the match begins. The opposition are unsurprisingly full of energy and seem to be playing in a flexible formation, meaning that their players aren't each sticking to one position and are hard to track.

You'll need to think smart to overcome this challenge and stay in control. Ten minutes into the first half, you have a throw-in close to the opposition's goal. You pause to decide where best to throw the ball in order to make sure the right player gets it. Players can't be offside from a throw-in, so you have more options open to you. Where should you aim the ball? You need to quickly work out who's in a useful position. To do this, on the area of the pitch shown on the opposite page, map out possible positions for players to receive the ball.

Place A, B, C and D once each into every row and column within the grid, with each letter representing a player. A player in a position labelled A is most likely to score from your throw-in, while a player in a position labelled D is least likely to score. The letters given outside the grid represent your analysis of the pitch and must match the nearest letter within their row/column. Letters can't share squares, so there will be exactly one empty square in every row and column.

Once you've placed every letter, look at the arrows indicating your options for the throw-in. You want to throw directly to a player in a position labelled A, so which of these three arrows is closest to such a position?

# AVAILABILITY

**Despite a promising start, the opposition's flexible formation style means that you're struggling to be in the right place at the right time. They've had most of the possession and have managed to net two goals in response to your throw-in success earlier in the match. When the whistle blows for half-time, your team are 2-1 down.**

In the dressing room, your manager urges you to focus on positioning and where the opposition players have been making themselves available, to ensure that they are well placed to intercept long passes. The boss is sure that this will be the key to disrupting their play and, to this end, has mapped out areas where the opposition are strongest, so that your team can better calculate where they need to place themselves in the second half.

Insert your players in some squares on the pitch on the opposite page to indicate where players in your team should be positioned. Numbered squares mark the positions of opposition players, with each number indicating how many players from your own team should be present within the same row and column combined in order to best counter them. Arrange your players on the pitch to follow these numerical requirements, while still ensuring that your play is balanced – just like you practised in training – so players should not be in adjacent or diagonally adjacent squares, either to those of their own or the opposing team.

⏱ **Can you work out these player positions in less than five minutes, before the second half begins? If you do, you've scored a penalty! If it takes you longer than ten minutes, the second half has already started. You're booked, and must turn to the Referee's Table on page 222.**

# LUCKY STRIKE

**For the first time in the second half, it's a goal! You were awarded a corner on the 80-minute mark and – to your great relief – one of your team-mates curled it neatly into the box, where it finally made it into the goal via a lucky deflection. But who scored it?**

There were plenty of people in the penalty box when the ball was sent over, and it's not clear who got the final touch. Can you determine whom the goal should be credited to from the map of the penalty box below?

Draw a series of separate paths between players, each connecting a pair of identically numbered players, to represent the routes from each player's starting position to their end position in the penalty area during the build up to the goal. No more than one path can enter any square, and paths can only travel horizontally or vertically between squares.

When you've joined up all the pairs, take a look at the final result. One of the paths will travel through the ball and tell you which player scored the goal. If the path that travels through the ball is between two even numbers, the goal was scored by your team! If it's odd, then it's the opposition's own goal – oops!

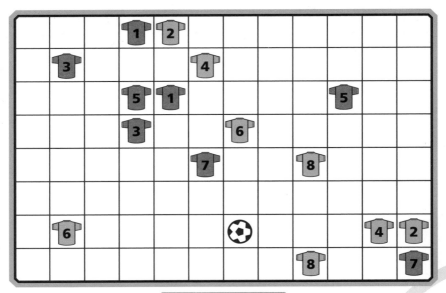

# EXTRA TIME

**The whistle blows for 90 minutes, but the score is still 2-2. Neither team can celebrate yet!**

After a ten-minute break, you're back on the pitch for extra time to see who can score again and go through to the semi-finals.

It's an absolute nail-biter and, after your tactical talk at half-time, the teams have seemed evenly matched. You need to quickly work out a way to boost your attacking chances, without giving the opposition too much of a shot at success.

Find your way through extra time on the visual representation of the ebb and flow of play drawn below, from kick-off on the

left to the final whistle on the right. If your path travels through an orange ball, it's a goal for your team. If it passes through a blue ball, however, you concede a goal. There are several ways you can get through the maze, so make sure you find the one that ends with you scoring more goals than the opposition!

Can you find a winning way through and make it to the semi-finals?

127

SOLUTION ON PAGE 209

# SEMI-FINALS

You've made it through to the semi-finals! You benefited from some decisive play in the final stages of the quarters, and a sparkling extra time in which your team defended well and saw off some serious threats from the opposition.

As always, there's a plan in place for the run-up to your semi-final. There are lessons to be learned, and time will be spent polishing tactics and techniques in the training sessions before your next big game. Expect loops, cones and plenty of player placement in the next few practice sessions. Your manager is looking for perfection, and only practice makes perfect!

# MESSY STRATEGY

Your backroom staff have been studying the opposition's last few matches closely. They think that there is an opportunity to be had if you can build from the back and thread the ball through to unlock their defence.

However, their plan was scrambled in the chaos of the dressing room, and you've only got a few minutes until training starts. Can you piece their tactics back together again in time to practise it out on the training pitch?

No pieces have been rotated more than 90 degrees, so they are all in the correct orientation to be inserted. Some pieces are identical, and so either of the identical pieces can go into the grid in one of two places.

## How did you score?

| ⏱ More than 20 minutes: You're booked! | ⏱ 16-20 minutes: Slow spectator | ⏱ 12-16 minutes: Average observer | ⏱ 10-12 minutes: Eagle-eyed | ⏱ Less than 10 minutes: Penalty scored! |

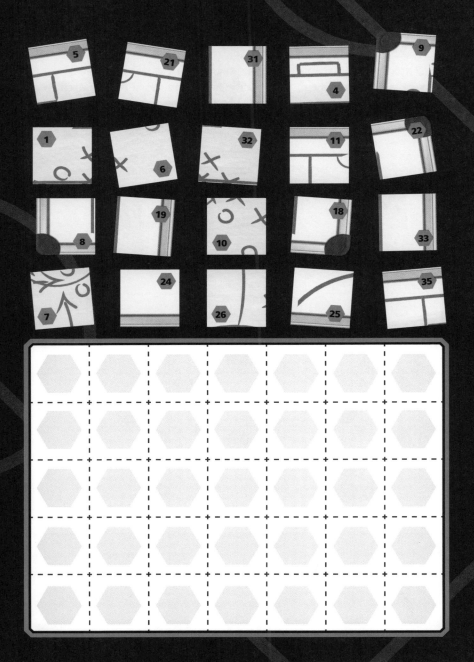

SOLUTION ON PAGE 209

# WARM-UP

**Your next game just might be the most important you've ever played, and you and the team will need to be more than match fit if you want to make it all the way to the final. In the run-up to the semi-finals, the training is going to be extra intense.**

Luckily, however, today's training session is one you'll be familiar with by now – although the coaching team have added in a few more obstacles.

Jog around the pitch by drawing a loop that visits every empty square, moving only horizontally or vertically between squares. The loop cannot enter any of the squares it has already visited, or any of those that contain training cones.

As usual, your speed will be monitored, so make your way around the pitch as quickly as you can without being reckless and making mistakes that you later need to undo. Compare your time against the scoreboard below.

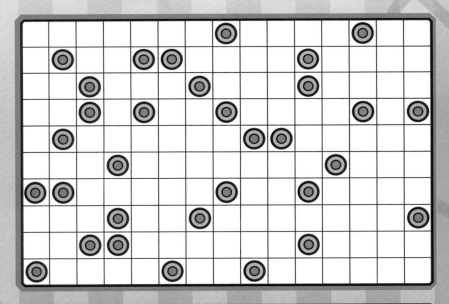

## How did you score?

| ⏱ Over 8 minutes: You're booked! | ⏱ 7-8 minutes: Slow sprinter | ⏱ 5-7 minutes: Average athlete | ⏱ 4-5 minutes: Swift striker | ⏱ Under 4 minutes: Penalty scored! |
|---|---|---|---|---|

SOLUTION ON PAGE 210

# NEGATIVE SPACE

**Even though you won your match in the quarter-finals, it was by no means an easy game.**

Players on the opposing team managed to keep much of the possession, meaning that your team rarely got a look-in, and it was mostly thanks to set pieces that you were able to make a mark on the scoreline.

In this training session, the aim of the game is possession. This time, your manager wants to demonstrate how negative space can be used to make sure that your team keep possession of the ball. "Negative space", in this case, means the space behind you – it's essentially passing backwards, towards your own goal, into less-defended space. You'll need to keep your passes short, however – a stray ball heading towards your own half is not something you want to take a chance on!

Practise passing the ball around the pitch below by writing a number in every empty square so that each number from 1 to 54 appears in the grid. Numbers must be placed so as to form a path from 1 to 54, in such a way that you can always move to an adjacent square one higher in value at each step. To better allow use of the negative space, in this case, "adjacent" also includes diagonally adjacent squares.

| | | 25 | 26 | | 28 | | 30 | |
|---|---|---|---|---|---|---|---|---|
| 22 | 21 | | | | | 29 | | 31 |
| | | 37 | 36 | | | | 1 | |
| | 38 | | | | | 13 | | 2 |
| | 54 | | | | | | 9 | |
| 53 | | 50 | 46 | 45 | | | | |

SOLUTION ON PAGE 210

# FILL THE GAPS

**Your next tactics session will also take place on the training pitch.**

There's a lot to learn from the mistakes of the quarter-final: the opposition's unpredictable positioning really left your team on the back foot.

 With man-marking, there's a risk that the opposition can force your team into unusual positions, and if one person loses their player, you are in trouble. Your manager wants to make sure that your team can learn to quickly fill any gaps that are created by an opposing team's unusual formation, so that you're not offering up easy chances for them to break through.

On the pitch below, some positions for players from both teams have been marked. Can you fill out the rest of the pitch with players, so that each square contains either a red player, representing the opposition, or a purple player, showing a player from your team? To ensure you close up the gaps, place them in such a way that no lines of four or more of either team are created in any direction, including diagonally. There need not be an equal number of players from both teams.

# MORE MAN-MARKING

**Instead of focusing on zonal marking, your manager wants man-marking to be a priority in the next game: it's essential that you don't let individual players from the opposition out of your sight.**

Can you practise your man-marking on the pitch below and prove to the boss that you can make sure everyone's in the right position when you're against the clock?

Draw an X to label a marking position next to each purple opposition player below, so that those rows and columns labelled with numbers contain that given number of marking positions. Unlabelled rows and columns can contain any number of positions.

Marking positions can only be placed in an empty square immediately above, below or to the side of an opposition player. To keep the formation balanced, two marking positions cannot be in touching squares – not even diagonally. Each marking position applies only to a single opposition player.

Time yourself. When you're done, compare your time against the scoreboard on the left.

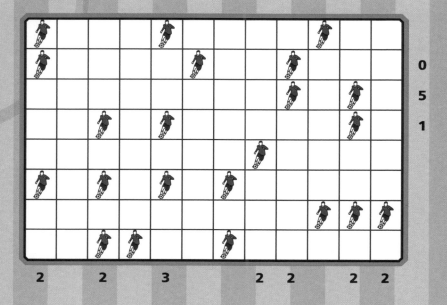

135

SOLUTION ON PAGE **211**

# EXHAUSTED TRACKING

In the last round, when the game went beyond 90 minutes, the mental fatigue really began to set in. Your manager noticed that the entire squad struggled with their attention to detail once you became tired, which is why you conceded. Fortunately, the other team struggled even more – perhaps they had not put in quite as many hours in training as you had.

With that in mind, the manager has come up with another attention-based exercise for you. Right after you come in from training – tired and looking forward to refuelling – the boss has you all sit down in front of a photo. Each of the players in it is reacting to the location of the ball, which has been removed from the image. Can you work out, from the positions and eyelines of the players shown, where the ball would be at the moment when the photo was taken?

Work out which square in the grid you think the ball should be in, and then make a note of that square's coordinates. Once you're done, see how well you did by comparing your choice against the scoreboard below. Trace a path from your square to the ball's real position, first with a horizontal line and then a vertical one. Then count how many squares – if any – are between your solution and the correct one.

## How did you score?

| 4 squares away: Another booking! | 3 squares away: Slow spectator | 2 squares away: Average observer | 1 square away: Eagle-eyed | Right on target: Penalty scored! |

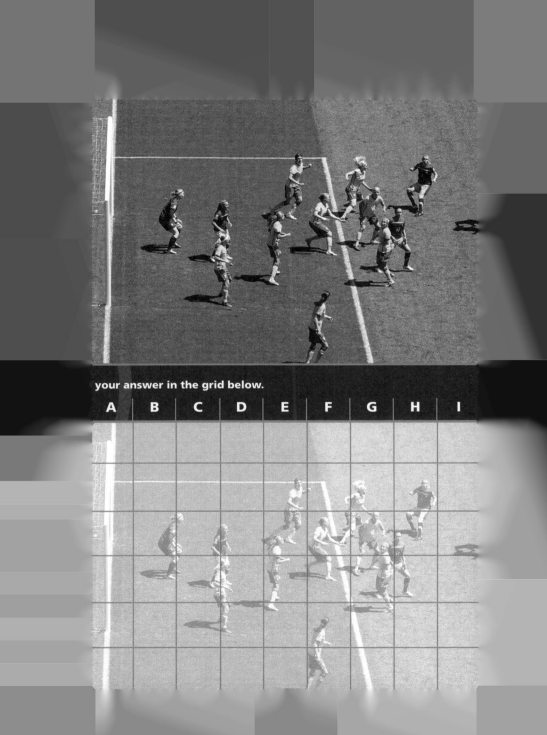

your answer in the grid below.

A B C D E F G H I

# CASE BY CASE

**The team you'll face in the semi-finals are well known for changing their formation and tactics on a game-by-game basis, depending on whom they're playing.**

They've done their homework on all the teams they've faced so far, so your match against them will be a real test. Unfortunately, it also means that you don't know exactly what style they'll be playing in. It's best for the team to be prepared for all eventualities. You'll need to practise different techniques and learn when to apply each one to have a chance of progressing.

In this training session, you'll keep an eye on the position of certain opposition players while making your way around the pitch and ensuring that you never approach too closely with the ball. You can use the data you have on individual players to make choices about how to negotiate your path around them. The lower the number, the more likely it is that that player will try to take the ball from you – so you want to spend less time in squares neighbouring that player.

Dribble the ball in a single loop through some empty squares, travelling using only horizontal and vertical lines between squares. Your loop must not cross or overlap itself and can only visit empty grid squares. Squares containing opposition players are marked with numbers, and the numbers indicate how many touching squares the loop passes through, including diagonally touching squares.

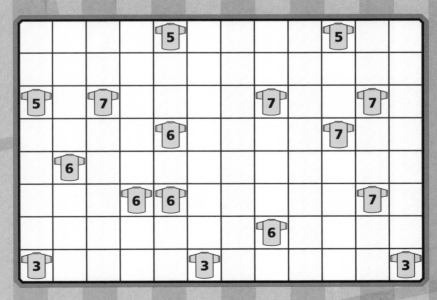

# RULE OF 6

**Whatever tactics the opposition use in the semi-finals, your manager wants your team to end up with the greater share of the possession so that they can control the flow of the game.**

The coaching staff want to revisit an exercise they devised back in the group stage, which they think will be a useful mental tool for the team going into the next match.

The challenge for the players is to make sure that the opposition are never allowed to have more than six consecutive touches of the ball before it's intercepted by one of your own team. The aim is to break up the momentum of the opposing players, so that they can't easily reach a goalscoring position.

On the sketch of the pitch below, your manager has drawn out a map of a hypothetical series of touches in different parts of the pitch. The touches in each area of possession have been numbered from 1 to 6. Can you separate the areas by drawing along some of the dashed grid lines, creating blocks that contain each of the numbers 1 to 6 only once?

| 4 | 1 | 3 | 3 | 5 | 1 | 4 | 3 | 1 |
|---|---|---|---|---|---|---|---|---|
| 2 | 3 | 6 | 2 | 4 | 6 | 6 | 2 | 4 |
| 4 | 1 | 4 | 5 | 1 | 2 | 5 | 2 | 3 |
| 5 | 6 | 1 | 5 | 6 | 2 | 5 | 6 | 1 |
| 1 | 6 | 3 | 2 | 3 | 6 | 5 | 4 | 3 |
| 5 | 2 | 4 | 5 | 6 | 4 | 1 | 2 | 3 |

SOLUTION ON PAGE **212**

# EXPOSING OPPOSITION

**Your next match will be physically tough, especially after your extra-time heroics, but you need to be prepared for a mental workout too. Given the opposition's varied tactics, the team will need to be ready to quickly read situations during the game.**

In this training session, you'll make your way around the pitch and use the clues to help you work out the opposition's positioning. To do this, you'll dribble the ball in a loop around the pitch, while detecting and avoiding defenders.

The loop cannot re-enter any square, and any empty squares that the loop does not visit must be shaded – this is where the opposition players are located. These shaded squares cannot touch, except diagonally. Arrows in some squares show the exact number of shaded squares in a given direction in their row or column. Not all shaded squares are necessarily identified with arrows, so keep your eyes peeled for hidden opposition players as you create your loop.

⏱ **Can you complete the loop and locate all the opposition players in less than five minutes? If so, you've scored a penalty! Take more than ten, though, and you're booked. Turn to the Referee's Table on page 222.**

|   |   |   | ◀0 |   |   |   |   |   |
|---|---|---|---|---|---|---|---|---|
|   |   |   |   |   | ◀0 |   |   |   |
| 1▶ |   |   |   |   |   |   |   |   |
|   |   |   | 0▶ |   |   | ▲0 |   |   |
|   | ▲0 |   |   |   |   |   | ◀0 |   |
|   |   |   |   | ◀0 |   |   |   |   |

# ONE-TOUCH VOLLEYS

**Now that the team are prepped to stay alert and monitor the opposition's unfolding strategy, you can explore what to do with the ball when you gain possession.**

You spent a while honing your heading early in the competition, and it certainly came in handy. In this training exercise, you'll practise volleying the ball – which is famously tricky both to master and to defend against when done well.

Outside the penalty box shown below are several players from your team, marked with labels, who are ready to launch the ball into the box, where your strikers are primed to volley home with power. Can you get your team-mates into the correct positions so that they can volley the ball successfully when it comes their way?

Draw diagonal lines across certain squares to represent players, with exactly one player per bold-lined region. The players must be placed so that a ball kicked into the grid from each lettered clue would then exit the grid *at the same letter* elsewhere, having been volleyed by the exact number of players indicated by the number next to the letter. Volleys always change the direction of the ball by 90 degrees, just like headers did previously. The same player can be used in more than one chain of volleys, but they must stay at the same diagonal for both balls.

SOLUTION ON PAGE **212**

# ZOOM IN ON THE SMALL THINGS

Your team have a deep understanding now, both of each other and of the match tactics that you want to apply from game to game. However, at this stage, it is the tiny details that can make all the difference between heartache and victory. Therefore, the manager has devised an exercise to get you to focus on every little thing that is happening around you.

Take a look at the picture below, and then at the zoomed-in images opposite. All but one has had a small alteration made to it. Can you discover which one it is?

## How did you score?

| ⏱ More than 7 minutes: You're booked! | ⏱ 5-7 minutes: Slow spectator | ⏱ 4-5 minutes: Average observer | ⏱ 3-4 minutes: Eagle-eyed | ⏱ Less than 3 minutes: Penalty scored! |

A

B

C

D

E

F

SOLUTION ON PAGE **213**

# USING BOTH SYSTEMS

**It's back to the drawing board – literally. The team have worked hard on improving their anticipation skills, and your manager is sure that they can now read the opposition well.**

Though you have practised man-marking, the players also have to remain flexible and continue to keep in mind both a specific zone of marking and a designated player when they make defensive choices.

The manager's assistants have drawn up a map of the midfield below, showing hypothetical zones to defend that they think the opposing team will put players into. Can you work out where you and your team-mates should position yourselves so that you can each mark one player, in one area?

Place players in certain squares so that each row, column and bold-lined region contains exactly two players, with each zone containing one from each team. Players should be spaced out, which means that they cannot be in neighbouring squares to one another – not even diagonally.

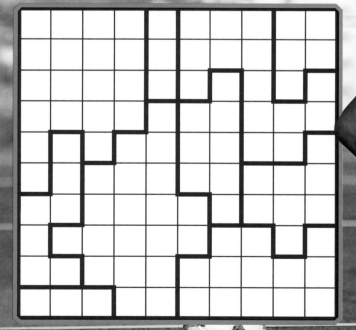

# LOOP THE LOOP

**It's the day before the semi-finals and tensions are running high. Although the team are feeling prepared after all of their training and tactics sessions, nerves are inevitable. The whole camp is jittery.**

Keen not to overwhelm the players with information before the big game, the coaching staff have set a simple loop-based exercise for this last training session. That said, it still involves some multitasking, so you won't be able to switch off completely!

Partially mapped out on the pitch below are the routes of six different loops for players to jog around the training pitch. To keep training organised, they need to be fully mapped out before the session begins, so some parts of the loops have been marked out already to act as a guide. Some training cones have also been put down, labelled with numbers, to mark particular squares that must be visited by a certain one of the six loops. Can you draw in the rest of the six looped routes?

Draw a set of six loops that together pass through all of the squares on the pitch, using all of the given fragments. In each square, a loop may pass straight through, turn 90 degrees or cross directly over another loop segment (either itself or another loop). Apart from in "crossing" squares, only one loop may enter any one square, and loops can never travel diagonally. Each loop must pass through at least one cone, and all cones with the same number must be part of the same loop and no other.

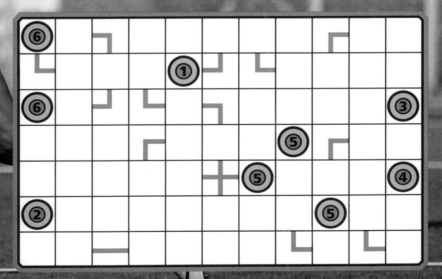

SOLUTION ON PAGE 213

# WINNING FORMATION

**In this final tactics session, you and the manager will put together the starting formation for the big semi-final.**

As captain, you've been trusted to take part in the exercise, not least because you'll be overseeing the team out on the pitch tomorrow, so you need to know where everyone should be! The boss wants to make sure every player knows exactly where they should be at all times, to remove as much doubt as possible from the game.

Shown on the right is a configuration for how the outfield players need to be grouped in sets.

As can be seen, there are six groups to place: three players in a line; two sets of neighbouring players; and three players on their own. Can you work out where you should place these six groups of players, according to the clues given on the half-complete tactics board below?

Mark the players in the grid, placing the groups so they run either horizontally or vertically between neighbouring squares. Different player groups cannot, however, be in touching squares – not even diagonally. Numbers outside the grid show the exact number of squares in their row or column that must be occupied by players. Three players are already placed.

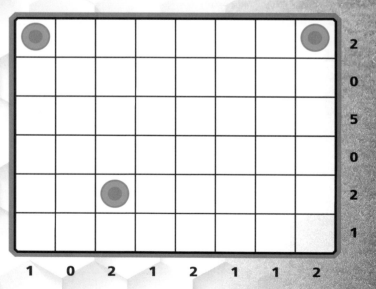

# HARD PRESS

At long last, you and the team are
heading out of the tunnel and into
the FIFA World Cup™ semi-final!
You've trained hard, taken in plenty
of tactical analysis, and now you're
ready to put it all to work on this high-
pressure international stage. As you line
up for the anthems, you know you've got what
it takes to earn the win and go through to the final!

As soon as the whistle blows, your team are immediately on the front foot
and eager to be the first to make a mark on the scoreboard. They're reading the
opposition well, and you're pleased to see they're pressing and attempting a lot of
interceptions to try to win possession. Can they turn their good intuition into goals?

On the field below, your players are represented by red shirts, and the opposition
by purple shirts. Map out a set of player paths that join each pair of identical
numbers. Paths can travel horizontally, vertically or diagonally between squares. No
more than one line can enter any square, but lines can cross if they do so diagonally
on the join between four squares.

If a path between two red shirts crosses a path between two purple shirts, your
team have managed to intercept the opposition – and will be able to score from
there. Once you've drawn in all the paths, take a look at the layout. How many of
these interceptions were achieved and, therefore, how many goals are scored?

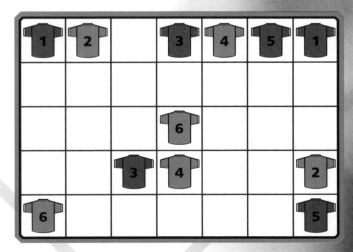

# GET TO THE END OF THE HALF

**Just before the half-time whistle blows, the opposition are awarded a corner. As they begin to position themselves in the penalty box, you want to make sure your players can block the incoming ball and clear it well outside of the area. If not, the opposition are likely to score.**

You have seven players back in the penalty box below, and you want to work out which potential position each player could take up in every row and column of the box, which has been divided into grid squares.

Representing players with digits from 1 to 7, place each digit once each into every row and column. These digits must be placed so that the numbers outside the grid give the total of the indicated diagonals.

You want to make sure none of the opposition players are able to get to the ball. Eventually, when the corner takes place, the ball is flighted into the box along the diagonal angle shown by the yellow arrow. Once you've worked out all the player positions, look at the marked diagonal. If its sum is greater than 30, the opposition will score. If it is 30 or fewer, no goal was scored. Do you manage to block them, or do they manage to score?

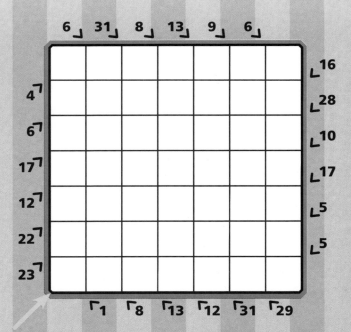

# LATE GOALS

**At the start of the second half, you're feeling pretty confident: there's still a good cushion between you and the opposition, and you are sure you can hold your nerve to secure the win.**

The other team, however, are fighting back hard. They rarely lose sight of the ball and, in the final 15 minutes of the game, create a lot of goalscoring opportunities. As players in both teams become more frantic, it's hard to keep up with the trajectory of play. Can you map out the final minutes of the game on the diagram below, and work out who manages to score late goals?

Add to the grid so that every square contains a number, and so that each number from 1 to 24 appears exactly once. Every number must be placed so that it is in a square whose arrow points in the direction of the next highest number. Your team's possession is represented by even numbers and the opposition's by odd numbers.

Boxes shaded in red mark the point from which a goal was scored; so, if the number in the box is even, it's a goal for your team – but if it's odd, you've conceded a goal.

When all the numbers are placed, which team scored more goals? Given that you were 4-1 up at half-time, what is the final score in the match?

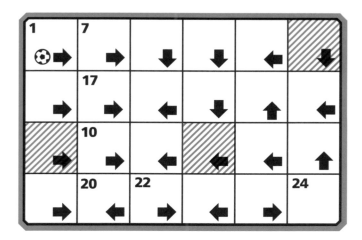

SOLUTION ON PAGE 215

# SPOT KICKS

**There are 30 minutes of extra time and – incredibly, given the eight earlier goals – neither team score. Despite their four goals each, neither side have yet done enough to make it through to the final. After some extremely defensive and cagey play, both your team and the opposition waited for an error from the other side which simply never came.**

As the whistle blows at the end of extra time, the players have to prepare for what comes next. It's the finale that none of you wanted: a penalty shoot-out.

You win the coin toss, which means your team will shoot first. After a brief huddle, your players gather on the halfway line, ready for the challenge. You'll need the penalty takers to

| | | | | | 1 | 1 | 1 | | | | 1 | 1 | 1 | |
|---|---|---|---|---|---|---|---|---|---|---|---|---|---|---|
| | | | 1 | 2 | 2 | 3 | 1 | | | 2 | 2 | 2 | 2 | 2 |
| | | | 3 | 3 | 3 | 2 | 4 | | | 4 | 3 | 3 | 3 | 1 |
| | | 10 | 1 | 1 | 1 | 1 | 2 | 10 | 10 | 2 | 1 | 1 | 1 | 2 | 10 |
| | | | 7 | 7 |
| | 1 | 1 | 2 | 2 |
| 1 | 5 | 1 | 3 | 1 |
| | 1 | 5 | 5 | 1 |
| | 1 | 3 | 2 | 2 |
| | 4 | 2 | 5 | 1 |
| | 5 | 1 | 5 | 1 |
| 5 | 1 | 1 | 3 | 1 |
| | 1 | 2 | 2 | 2 |
| | | | 7 | 7 |

**Your score**

**Opposition's score**

pick up on subtle clues from the keeper so that they can place the ball in an unreachable spot. Can you use the clues below to place pieces that reveal the final score of the shoot-out?

Shade some squares by obeying the clue constraints at the start of each row or column. The clues provide, in reading order, the length of every run of consecutive shaded squares in each row and column. There must be a gap of at least one empty square between each run of shaded squares in the same row or column.

Once you're done, the shoot-out score will be revealed. Your team's score is on the left, and the opposition's is on the right. So, who won on penalties?

# THE FINAL

This is it! After a gruelling semi-final, your team have made it all the way through to the final – congratulations! A nail-biting win in the penalty shoot-out meant that you were finally able to claim victory in a hard-fought match that tested both teams to the limit.

Your next match will be the biggest game of your life – not that you need reminding – so the coaching staff will leave no stone unturned in making sure you're fully prepared. More tactics sessions are on the way, along with some familiar warm-ups to get you ready for the big game. But with only a small amount of time left before the FIFA World Cup™ final, there's no time like the present to get back on the pitch and into the swing of things.

# QUIET JOG

Although you're exhausted from that full-on semi-final, the whole team are straight back on the pitch for more training sessions. As usual, you'll be tested on your speed, and this particular warm-up will also involve some colour-coded coordination – so you'll need to make sure you're paying attention as you make your way around the pitch.

Jog around the pitch in a single loop that passes over the centre of every cone, using only horizontal and vertical lines. The loop must pass in a straight line over every yellow cone, then make a 90-degree turn in one or both of the preceding and following squares. Conversely, the loop must make a 90-degree turn at every purple cone, but then travel straight through both the preceding and following squares without turning. The loop cannot visit any square more than once but does not need to visit every square.

🕐 **Don't forget: your speed is being recorded. Can you complete your loop in less than three minutes to score a penalty?**

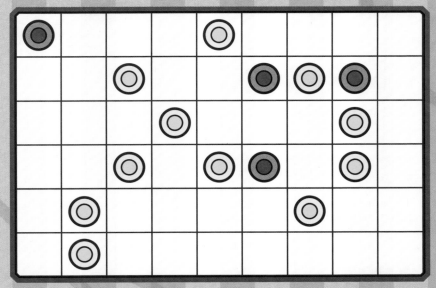

# SWITCH THE SPACE

**In the final, you have a rematch against the only team you've lost to so far, way back in the group stage.**

You've both won all your matches since then, and now you'll meet again in the final. Your manager wants to make sure that any errors from that game have since been corrected, and so starts today's tactics session by looking at how to switch up play and respond quickly when opposing players make mistakes.

The boss is pleased with your work on reading the opposition and thinks the players are in the right mindset to take every opportunity to intercept the ball. Successful interceptions need to be acted on quickly, however, with the player who wins possession counter-attacking in a clear line towards the goal while the opposition are still on the back foot. It's all about rapidly switching path to make the most of the change in momentum, and quickly focusing one's attention on the new direction of play.

On the map of the pitch below are nine of your team's players. Can you show, based on their location, how much space these players have to switch their positioning so they're better able to counter-attack?

Draw along some of the grid lines to divide the grid into a set of regions, so every grid square is in exactly one region. Every region must contain exactly one player, and the region must be symmetrical in such a way that, if rotated 180 degrees around the player, it would look exactly the same.

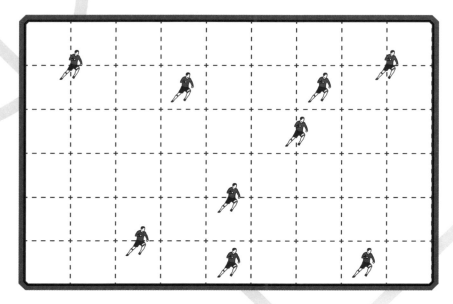

SOLUTION ON PAGE **216**

# ASSURED LINES

**After the tactics session, it's time to put your thinking into action. You've demonstrated how you can switch up your momentum quickly if you or your team-mates manage to intercept the ball.**

In this training exercise, decisive movement is the name of the game. As soon as you intercept, you'll need to create a clear and calculated path down the pitch with the ball, so that you can really capitalise on your opponents' mistake and mount a swift counter-attack.

Can you show your manager that you're able to calculate your paths quickly? Draw a loop that visits every square once, travelling only horizontally or vertically between squares. The loop can only enter and exit each bold-lined region once, so there's no going back on yourself once you've chosen a path.

Pace yourself. Mistakes will cost you precious seconds. Set a stopwatch and see if you can complete the loop inside two minutes. Fortunately, the boss is going easy to save your legs before the final, and so there is no penalty if you can't do it in the allotted time, as long as you get it right, of course.

# ANGLED SET PIECES

**Successful execution of set pieces has proven to be the key to some of your wins in the competition, so your manager wants to tick every box in the preparation for the final.**

In previous tactics sessions, a lot of work has been done on finding the right angle to send in the ball, whether from a free kick, corner or throw-in. In this session, you'll be looking at player placement in the penalty box, making sure that all bases are covered if a corner is awarded to your team.

The opposition's tactic for defending corners seems to be to crowd the box, to try to ensure that there's no clear path for the ball to reach your players. Your manager wants to counteract this by making sure your players are well spread out when you have a corner, so that the opposition have to make a choice between marking a specific player or filling the playing space. The idea, according to the boss, is to create space in the box so that a well-placed ball is more likely to have a clean path onto someone's head. Simple enough! Can you work out a way to spread out your players so that they are each able to cover equal amounts of space in the penalty area? Draw along some of the dashed grid lines on the pitch in order to divide the penalty area into four regions. The regions must all be identical, although they may be rotated (but not reflected) relative to one another.

159

SOLUTION ON PAGE **217**

# LIFT THE TROPHY

**Your squad have all long dreamed of lifting the trophy and are now on the verge of fulfilling that ultimate ambition. However, you are worried that they are getting a bit ahead of themselves.**

You walk into the dressing room to find your team-mates all acting out the moment that they hope will begin the celebrations after the match – hoisting the trophy high above their heads. While you are amused, you know that you need to ensure that they stay focused, or else the dream will stay just that: a dream.

In order to test that they are concentrating, you set them a task. Can you help them determine which of the images labelled A-D matches the image above precisely? Three of them have a small difference. If you cannot find the correct image within four minutes, you are booked and must turn to the Referee's Table on page 222.

# STAY ON TRACK

**When making a break towards the goal with the ball, you'll need to be ready to change direction if a defender gets in your way.**

To keep possession of the ball, you must stay on your feet while weaving a path around the opposition. Agility and speed need to go hand in hand if you want to make a success of a dangerous run – and this training exercise will be a test of both.

On the pitch below, the coaching staff want you to run in a loop that visits *every* square just once and does not cross itself. Training cones have been set out to show some of the places where you'll need to change direction. In fact, exactly half of the turns are already marked out: the cones show where every *second* turn in your loop must be located. So, in other words, you'll alternate between turning in a square *without* a cone and turning in a square *with* a cone.

Set a timer when you begin mapping out your path and then, when you're done, compare your time against the scoreboard below.

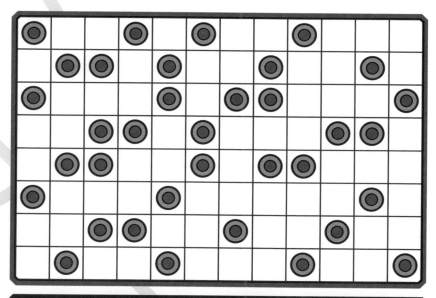

| How did you do? | | | | |
|---|---|---|---|---|
| ⏱ Over 10 minutes: You're booked! | ⏱ 7-10 minutes: Slow sprinter | ⏱ 5-7 minutes: Average athlete | ⏱ 4-5 minutes: Nifty negotiator | ⏱ Under 4 minutes: Penalty scored! |

SOLUTION ON PAGE **217**

# INFORMATION OVERLOAD

**It's rare for two teams to meet twice in a FIFA World Cup™, so it's unlucky for you that, in the final, you'll be facing the only team to beat you so far.**

You know your whole team have improved enormously over the last few games, however, and you're hoping that any previous issues were ironed out in the training and tactics sessions during the knockout stage.

One of the problems that led to your defeat was sharing information. In the frenzy of the game, it was difficult to understand the instructions from the coaching staff, your manager and even your team-mates over the noise of the crowd – which you know will be even louder this time. As practice for dealing with this, use the clues given from the sidelines below to create the intended path from A to B across the pitch.

Shade some squares to form a single path that starts at A and ends at B. It must be a path formed of touching squares that does not branch off or cross over itself. Your route also cannot bend back on itself and visit a square that touches another square in the route at any point – not even diagonally, except when turning a corner. The coaching staff's clues are indicated by numbers outside the grid, with each clue specifying the number of squares in its row or column that are visited by the route, including the squares labelled A and B. If there's no number, the route can visit any number of squares in that row or column. The route can only move horizontally or vertically from square to touching square.

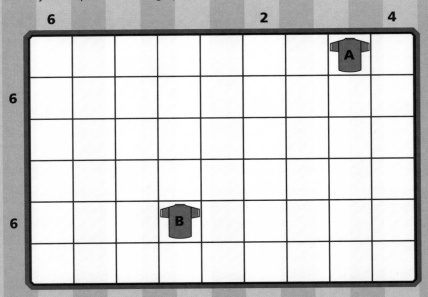

# BALANCING ACT

**Your manager is convinced that quick reactions are going to be the key to winning this final.**

There's no point in the players being match fit if they can't take advantage of their physical speed because of a failure to respond rapidly to an unfolding situation on the pitch. They must be able to look at the game on two levels simultaneously, with an awareness of the fine details of the game balanced by an ability to see the big picture and make decisions based on the player positions across the whole pitch.

This exercise involves looking at the pitch on those two levels. On the one hand, you need to make sure there's no immediate overcrowding in any one area. On the other, you'll have to pay attention to areas of the pitch that may be some distance from your immediate focus, so that you obey the rules for each row and column.

On the pitch below, some players from both teams have been marked in – your team with purple shirts and the other with yellow. Fill the rest by placing a shirt in each empty square, so that there is an equal number of each colour within every row and every column. To make sure there's no overcrowding, there must be no more than two of the same colour in succession when reading along any row or column.

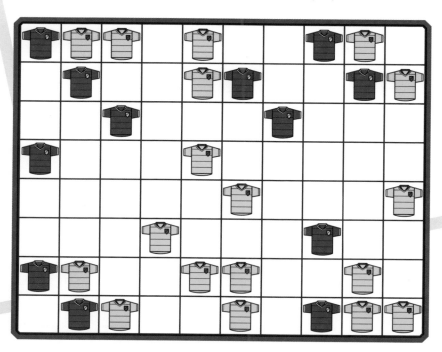

SOLUTION ON PAGE **218**

# EMPTY SPACE

**Based on the team's performance in the semi-finals, your manager wants to make sure that players are ready to take decisive action whenever they get the ball.**

You've already spent some time practising breakthrough runs and mapping out a path between you and the goal when you have the ball, but you must not neglect passing. It's one of the most essential skills you'll need to use on the pitch, and now seems like the right time to perfect the basics.

In this exercise, accuracy is the name of the game. On the pitch below, you'll be passing the ball into empty space – but only according to the directions given. You'll need to work out exactly where the receiving player is going to be before you pass, to make sure there are no stray balls that might leave you open to interception.

Each of the numbers represents one touch of the ball on the way to the goal. Add numbers to the grid so that every square contains a number and each number from 1 to 23 appears exactly once. Every number must be in a square whose arrow points in the direction of the next highest number, except for 23 which must be in a square that points at the goal. Your route will end at the goal, which is marked for you.

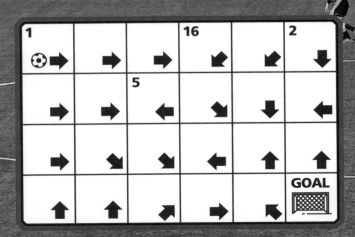

# SPEED TEST

**In the semi-finals, your team had to play on for an extra 30 minutes after the second half, before then going on to win on penalties.**

Having given it their all for the full 120 minutes, however, the players were exhausted. Unsurprisingly, the coaching staff want to make sure that everyone has recovered and is as fit as possible for the final – although, this time, you're hoping to have won by the 90-minute mark!

Set out on the training pitch below are several training cones. Can you create a loop that allows you to run around the entire pitch without crossing over your own path or revisiting a cone? To do so, draw lines that connect all of the cones in a loop to show your path, using only horizontal or vertical lines. Some of the loop has already been filled in.

This is a test of speed, so start a timer before you begin drawing your loop. This loop is harder to create than some you have encountered earlier and will require some experimentation to find the solution.

⏱ **If you completed the exercise within ten minutes, congratulations! You have scored a penalty. If you took longer than 20 minutes, then you received a card, and you must turn to the Referee's Table on page 222.**

SOLUTION ON PAGE **219**

# HARD TO FIND

Time is now short until your last challenge, and every moment is being spent preparing. However, the very worst thing that you could do when you are so close to being ready would be to overtrain and fatigue yourself, or worse, put yourself at risk of injury. On the other hand, your mental training contains no such concerns, and you are spending hours holed up with the boss, poring over the tiniest details of the opposition's game in order to find an edge.

With that in mind, the manager has come up with another exercise for you, having picked out an image in which an entire team of 11 players are situated inside the penalty area, desperately defending – a situation which might come up in the final, and which causes maximum chaos. Each of the players in it is reacting to the location of the ball, which has been removed from the image. Can you work out, from the positions and eyelines of the players shown, where the ball would be at the moment when the photo was taken?

Work out which square in the grid you think the ball should be in, and then make a note of that square's coordinates. Once you're done, see how well you did by comparing your choice against the scoreboard below. Trace a path from your square to the ball's real position, first with a horizontal line and then a vertical one. Then count how many squares – if any – are between your solution and the correct one.

## How did you score?

| 4 squares away: Another booking! | 3 squares away: Sloppy spectator | 2 squares away: Average observer | 1 square away: Eagle-eyed | Right on target: Penalty scored! |

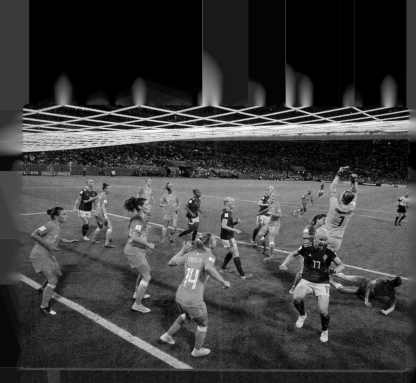

your answer in the grid below.

| A | B | C | D | E | F | G | H | I |
|---|---|---|---|---|---|---|---|---|

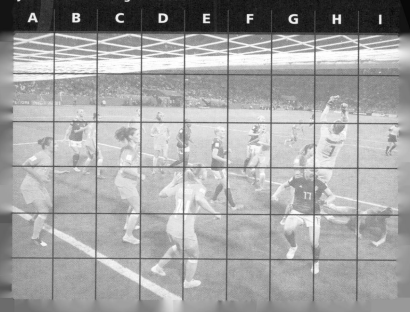

# MARKING AT THE DOUBLE

**Your manager has been reviewing your upcoming opposition, particularly the previous match you two played, in which they came out victorious.**

The boss and backroom staff have noticed that, on top of man-marking, the other team seem to be taking it one step further and have occasionally doubled up with two of their players marking one attacker that they think is especially dangerous with the ball. Can you use the clues below to work out which of your players might be marked by two opponents, based on the stats you have been given? This will allow you to have them chasing shadows by passing to a player left unmarked.

On the pitch below, your players have been valued according to how effective they are at converting possession into goalscoring opportunities. In this case, the higher the numbers, the more effective the players – that means they'll have a

greater chance of being marked by two opponents within a single grid-square area.

Place one or two opposition players into some empty squares according to the numbers on your team's players. Each number shows the total number of opponents in touching squares, including diagonally touching squares. No more than two players may be placed in any square.

# FINAL COUNTDOWN

**It's your last training session before the FIFA World Cup™ final! After months of hard work, miles of running in loops, and more training cones than you could ever count, you're almost ready for what you hope will be the greatest game of your life. No pressure!**

In this final session, you'll draw together techniques you've been working on since your very first training sessions in the qualifying rounds, multitasking to the best of your abilities and making sure your team stick together. Can you find a path around the pitch below that will allow you to dribble the ball from one cone to another, while also blocking off the markers representing opposition players?

On the pitch below, your team-mates are the players in purple, and the opposition markers are shown in yellow. Draw a single loop on the pitch by connecting some of the cones, so that each number shown in the grid is adjacent to that many line segments. Diagonal connections aren't allowed, and the loop cannot cross itself or revisit a cone. All players in your team must be situated inside the loop, and all opposition players must be outside it.

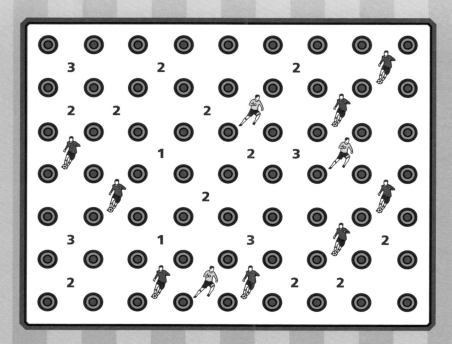

SOLUTION ON PAGE 220

# PASSING INTO SPACE

**In your final tactics session before the big game, your manager wants you and the team to take an in-depth look at a possible scenario involving passing ahead of each other's runs.**

This kind of through-ball can be used to great advantage – especially against a team employing a man-marking system – if one of your team can shake the defence loose with an abrupt, well-timed run. On the other hand, if you pass to the wrong place, your ball might end up being easily picked up by the opposition.

In the scenario below, there are four possible squares a ball can be passed into, each marked with a football. Can you quickly assess which position is the only one that can be reached by one of your team's players?

Each of the numbered boxes below represents somewhere a player might be – purple shirts are your team, and yellow shirts are the opposition. To work out which player would reach each ball, draw one or more horizontal or vertical lines travelling away from the players to show the squares they are covering. The various players' numbers tell you how many grid squares their lines travel into, although the player squares themselves do not count toward this total. Lines shouldn't enter or cross over squares

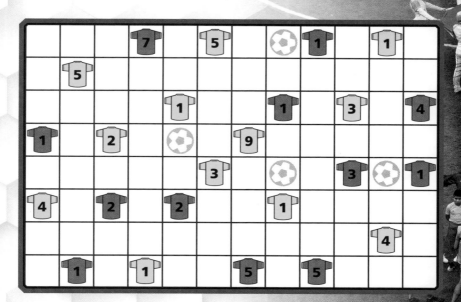

containing other players, nor enter a square containing a line coming from another player. When you are finished, every non-player square will have a line in it. Check back to a similar exercise the manager had you do in the qualifying stages for an example if needed.

If a line passes through one of the balls, it means the player connected to that line will be able to reach it. Of the four places the ball can be passed to, which one should be chosen so that it can be reached by a player from your team?

THE FINAL

# KICK-OFF

**You've made it… it's the FIFA World Cup™ final!**

**As you lead your team out of the tunnel and on to the pitch, the sound of thousands of fans roars in your ears, not to mention the unheard thunder of untold millions watching the match on TV all over the world. Lining up for the national anthem, you feel ready for the biggest game of your life. You've trained for hours, covered every angle of tactical analysis, and won many tough matches against some of the best teams in the world. And now, in just 90 minutes, you might be the world champions.**

The first half – as you would expect – is an exciting one. Both sets of players are hugely energetic and the pace of the match is hard to keep up with, so it's a good job you've been working on your fitness. Both teams create great chances in the first 45 minutes, so can you work out who's ahead when the whistle blows for half-time?

The pitch below provides an incomplete map of some of the significant corners, throw-ins, free kicks and passes from the first half. Four of them have resulted in goals, marked by the four stars on the pitch. Work out who scored which goals by drawing a series of separate paths, each connecting a pair of identical numbers. No more than one path can enter any square, and paths can only travel horizontally or vertically between squares.

This has truly been football in the round so, in this puzzle, the paths may also run off one side of the pitch. Wherever they do, the same path will continue on the opposite side of the pitch. In other words, paths can "wrap around" from one side of the pitch to the other. Part of one path from the 5 is shown to make this clear, continuing on the opposite side of the pitch.

Whenever a path crosses through a star, it's a goal: if the path is between two purple numbers, it's a goal for your team; if it's a yellow path, however, it means the opposition have scored. So, when the whistle blows for half-time, what's the score?

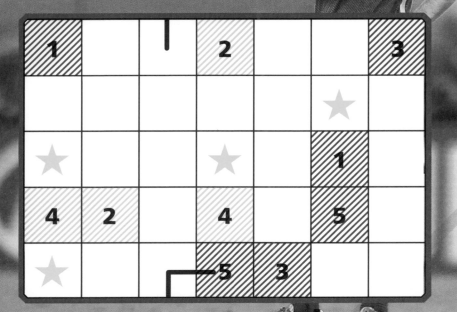

# HALF-TIME

**In the dressing room, the air is full of nervous energy. Never one to miss a teachable moment, your manager draws the team together for a final strategy discussion, to demonstrate a possible way of turning the opposition's tactics against them.**

The opposing team are playing a wide game, and they're relying on long, high cross-field passes to switch play. In theory, these are difficult to intercept – it's something you've practised yourself in training – but your manager has a plan.

Given that you're all far more than ordinarily match fit, you can exploit your stamina to gain an advantage. To do this, when defending you must move into empty spaces when the opposition is least expecting it. In that way, because you are defensively out of position, you can lead the opposition into a false sense of security, so that they pass the ball lower to the ground. It's then that you use your fitness and agility to suddenly sprint so that you can appear at the last moment to intercept. Can you prove to the boss that you'll be able to work out where to run to in the scenario below?

Add purple shirts to certain squares to mark target locations for defenders from your team. Each yellow-shirted attacker is labelled with a number showing the total number of target locations to place in its row and column. No two shirts can be in touching squares – not even diagonally.

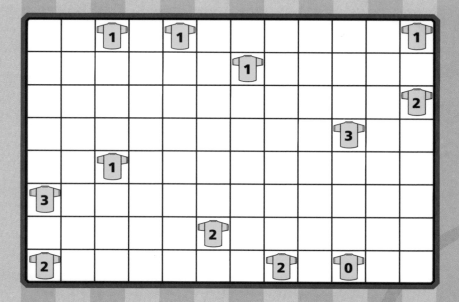

# DEFLECT AND DEFEND

**Now is the time to put your manager's ploy into action by disrupting the opposition's long passes and, in turn, their game plan.**

The whistle blows and your players start to work out their positioning for the second half. They need to be able to intercept long passes and deflect them away from their original path. The field below represents this. Can you work out where to place your players so that every attack by an opponent makes no progress?

These attacks start at a letter and then end at the same letter elsewhere on the field. Add your players so that *every* attack is thwarted in such a way, by marking the squares where players should deflect the ball. To do so, draw diagonal lines from corner to corner in certain squares to indicate your players, with exactly one player per bold-lined region. They should be placed so that, when lines are drawn directly into the grid from any letter, they deflect off one or more players back out of the grid to the matching letter. Deflections always turn the ball through 90 degrees, as indicated by the direction of the diagonal, and the number of deflections each path takes is marked after the letter, so A4 will take 4 deflections. Some players will deflect balls coming at them from two different directions, but they must stay at the same diagonal for both balls.

Passes fly over most of the field. How many squares are *never* visited by balls?

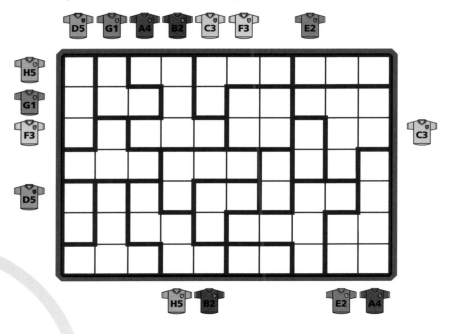

SOLUTION ON PAGE **221**

# NOW OR NEVER

**You've managed to defend some of the difficult balls that came your way at the beginning of the second half – but it's not over yet. The score is 2-2 but, with your side struggling to create credible chances of your own, the opposition seem to have the advantage over you.**

The clock ticks on and you're into the final 30 minutes of the match. Drawing upon all your mental reserves, you remind yourself that you and your team definitely have the skill, energy and training to turn things around and claim a victory. But the other team seem to have had a similar thought about their lack of threat, and now both teams are throwing everything they have into their attacking play.

Mapped out on the field are some of the positions the players find themselves in during this last stage of the final, with each of the numbered shirts representing a player's position. Join these positions with passes from player to player, with each pass represented as a horizontal or vertical line. The ball must be passed from each shirt as many times as is specified by the value. No more than two passes may join any pair of positions and, crucially, no passes may cross one another or pass over a player's position. The finished layout must connect all positions, so that you can pass the ball from one position to any other simply by following one or more lines.

Can you get the ball into the opponent's goal at the top of the page, while defending your own at the bottom? Each vertical "shot" – represented by a line between shirts – crossing into each of the goal areas is a goal scored by the team attacking that way. It's a nail-biting – and very high-scoring – final 30 minutes. But when the whistle blows, what's the final score, given that it was 2-2 going into this?

**Have you done enough to lift the trophy?**

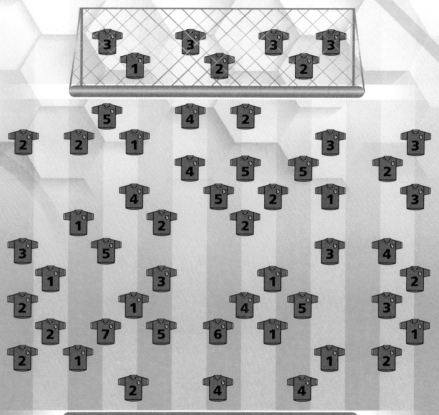

YOUR GOAL

177

# SOLUTIONS

**Warm-up**

**Balancing Bibs**

**Training Cones**

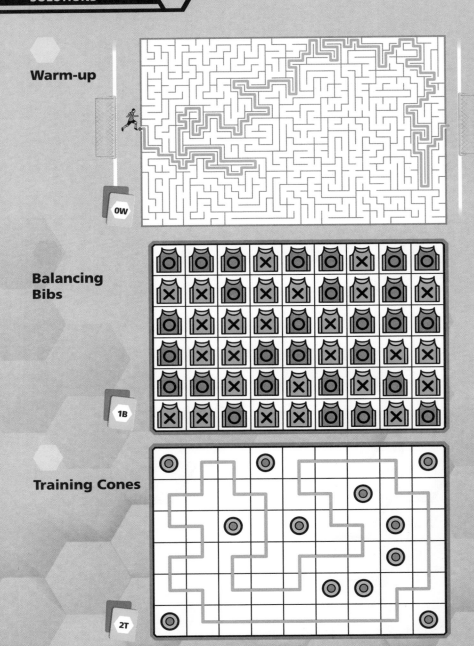

## Inside the Box

The manager has marked out 38 rectangles on the pitch – so there must be 38 members of the squad in this session.

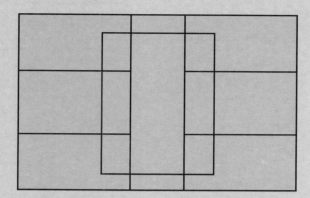

**3I**

## Precise Perception

**4P**

## Defensive Match

**6D**

## Pitch Possession

Six players are covering the striped area. The manager speaks to each of them individually, and motivates them for the second half.

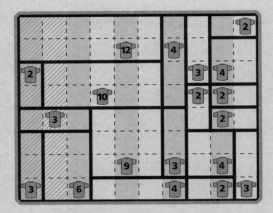

**7P**

## Goalscorers

You're in luck – your team scored all three goals! Two of them went to one striker, and one to you. That makes the final score 3-1 to your team. You've won your first match!

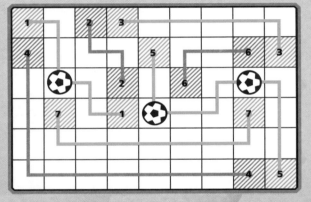

**8G**

## Warm-up

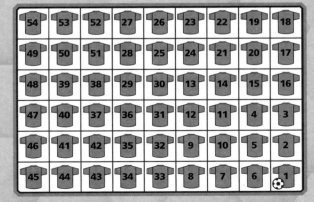

**9W**

182

**Set-piece
Perception**

0S

**Defence
Delegation**

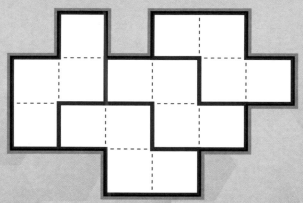

2D

**Speed-passing
Loop**

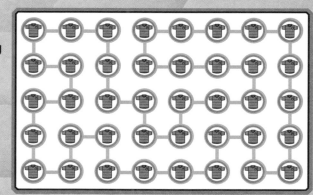

3S

### On-field Observation

40

### Penalty Box Positioning

6P

### Opportunities

You're in luck! Your number 9 is available to get the ball. You thread the ball through and your team-mate scores. You're 1-0 up!

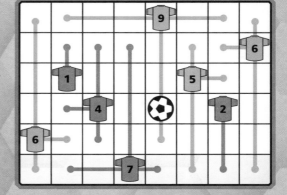

70

184

## Final Whistle

Your team score two of the three goals, with the other team scoring just one. It's another match that ends 3-1 to your team, which means you've won the second qualifier!

**8F**

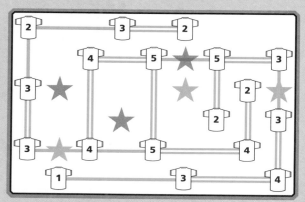

## Ball Tracking

**0B**

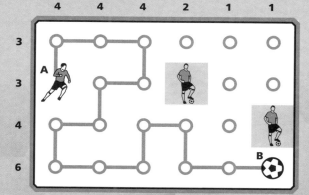

## Zonal Marking

**1Z**

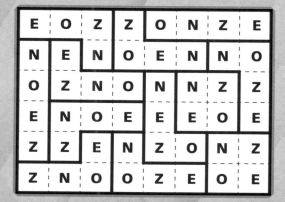

185

## Anticipation Check

**2A**

## Indirect Routes

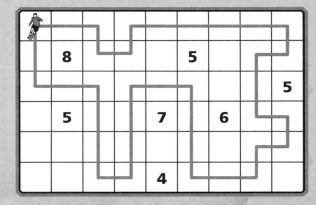

**4I**

## Cross-field Passing

There are six places where the cross-field passes cross one another.

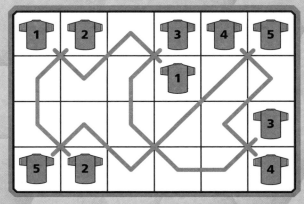

**5C**

## Breakthrough Lines

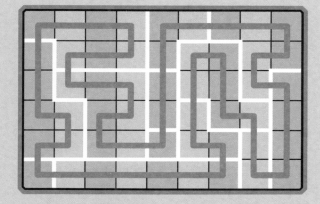

6B

## In Touch

Unfortunately, two of the goals are scored on blue paths, and only one on an orange path. That means the score is 2-1 to the opposition at half-time.

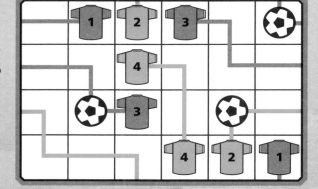

7I

## Playmaker

You've scored one goal – and managed to hold off the opposition and stop them from scoring. The final score is 2-2, which is enough to take you through to the group stage! Turn to the next page to read the epilogue.

8P

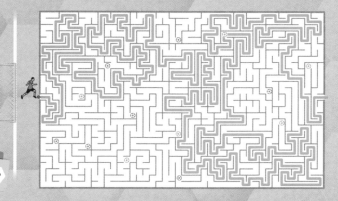

# CHAPTER 1 EPILOGUE

**CONGRATULATIONS** – you've officially qualified for a place in the FIFA World Cup™! You'll progress through to the group stage next and face the top teams from all over the world. With two wins and a draw, your team are pleased with their achievements in qualifying, and eager to prove they can achieve even more. Your manager certainly picked the right captain, and is counting on you to lead the squad against even fiercer competition.

But for now, sit back, relax and enjoy the moment!

**Running Drills**

2R

**Thinking Together**

E1

4T

## Star Scorer

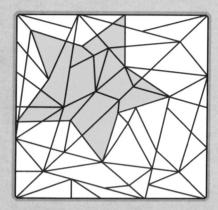

**6S**

## Circuit Training

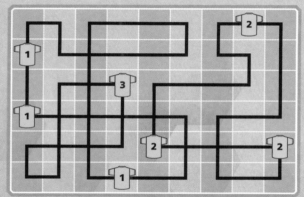

**7C**

## The Art of Flick-ons

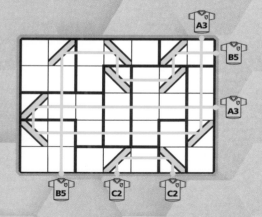

**8T**

## Sidelines

The arrow labelled A is the only one which points to a diagonal containing only even numbers.

9S

|  10⌐ | 17⌐ | 9⌐ | 8⌐ | 5⌐ |  | A  B |
|---|---|---|---|---|---|---|
| 2 | 1 | 4 | 3 | 6 | 5 | ⌐18 |
| 1 | 6 | 3 | 4 | 5 | 2 | ⌐4 |
| 4 | 5 | 6 | 2 | 3 | 1 | ⌐16 |
| 3 | 4 | 2 | 5 | 1 | 6 | ⌐5 |
| 6 | 2 | 5 | 1 | 4 | 3 | ⌐4 |
| 5 | 3 | 1 | 6 | 2 | 4 | |

2⌐ 2⌐ 14⌐ 14⌐ 26⌐ (row labels)

⌐5 ⌐9 ⌐6 ⌐19 ⌐11

C
D

## Indirect Free Kick

The middle of the three arrows points directly to a player labelled A – so that's the way you should kick the ball.

OI

## VAR

Great news! After a review, it's clear that the ball is completely over the line. The goal is awarded to your team, making the score 2-0. The final whistle blows and you've won the match!

1V

## Quick Loop

## Find the Defenders

There are seven defenders hidden in the grid.

| 1 | 2 | | 2 | | |
|---|---|---|---|---|---|
| | | 4 | | | 2 |
| | | | 2 | 3 | |
| | 1 | 2 | | | |

## Dribbling Drills

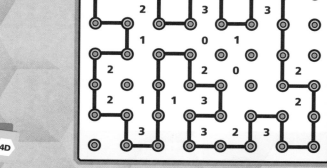

## Missing Something

H4

6M

Grid columns: A B C D E F G H I
Grid rows: 1 2 3 4 5 6

## Offensive Defence

8O

| 4 | 2 | 6 | 3 | 5 | 1 | 5 | 6 |
|---|---|---|---|---|---|---|---|
| 5 | 2 | 6 | 3 | 3 | 1 | 4 | 2 |
| 3 | 6 | 6 | 1 | 5 | 2 | 4 | 1 |
| 1 | 4 | 2 | 4 | 5 | 3 | 4 | 5 |
| 1 | 4 | 5 | 1 | 3 | 4 | 2 | 2 |
| 3 | 6 | 2 | 1 | 3 | 6 | 5 | 6 |

## Loop Logistics

9L

| 2 |  |  | 4 |  |  | 4 |  |  |
|---|---|---|---|---|---|---|---|---|
|  |  |  |  |  |  |  |  |  |
|  |  |  |  |  | 5 |  |  |  |
|  |  |  |  |  |  |  |  | 3 |
|  |  |  | 4 | 2 |  |  |  |  |
|  |  |  |  |  |  |  |  |  |

## Touchline Instructions

Unfortunately, the situation has been misread and your path crosses a square containing a defender. The opposing player takes the ball from you and scores. You're now 1-0 down.

**0T**

|  | 4 | 2 | 5 | 2 | 3 | 4 | 3 | 4 |
|---|---|---|---|---|---|---|---|---|
| **5** |  |  | ◯ | ◯ | ◯ | ◯ | A | |
| **1** |  |  | ◯ | | | | | |
| **7** | ◯ | ◯ | ◯ | | B | ◯ | ◯ | ◯ |
| **2** | ◯ | | | | | | | ◯ |
| **6** | ◯ | | ◯ | ◯ | ◯ | ◯ | | ◯ |
| **6** | ◯ | ◯ | ◯ | | | ◯ | ◯ | ◯ |

## Odds and Evens

It's not good news: the opposition have scored three goals and your team only managed to net one. When the final whistle goes, the score is 4-1 to the opposition. It's your first defeat in the FIFA World Cup™ campaign: hopefully, it's also your last.

**2O**

| 1 ⬇ | 19 ➡ | 20 ➡ | 18 ⬅ | 21 ➡ | 22 ⬇ |
|---|---|---|---|---|---|
| 2 ➡ | 9 ⬇ | 4 ⬇ | 7 ➡ | 3 ⬅ | 8 ⬅ |
| 12 ⬇ | 10 ➡ | 11 ⬅ | 17 ⬆ | 16 ⬅ | 23 ⬇ |
| 13 ➡ | 14 ➡ | 5 ➡ | 6 ⬆ | 15 ⬆ | 24 ⚽ |

## Man-Marking

**3M**

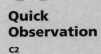

## Quick Observation

C2

4Q

## Tight Blocking

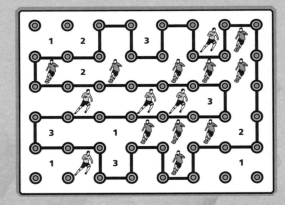

6T

## Up Front

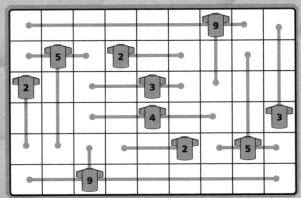

7U

## Interception

The player can be intercepted at point B.

81

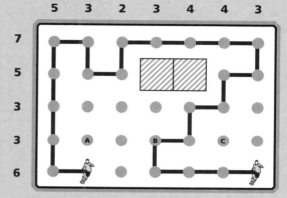

## Close Attention

D2

0C

## Free Kick

The arrow labelled B points to a column where 4 is visible from that point, so the free kick should be played in this direction. It's pinpoint accurate and your central defender rises tall and scores! The score is now 1-0 to you.

2F

| | 2 | 1 | 3 | 4 | 2 | |
|---|---|---|---|---|---|---|
| 2 | 4 | 5 | 3 | 2 | 1 | 4 |
| 3 | 2 | 1 | 4 | 3 | 5 | 1 |
| 1 | 5 | 2 | 1 | 4 | 3 | 3 |
| 3 | 3 | 4 | 5 | 1 | 2 | 2 |
| 3 | 1 | 3 | 2 | 5 | 4 | 2 |
| | 3 | 3 | 2 | 1 | 2 | |
| | | A | B | C | | |

## Shots on Target

Looks like all your hard work pays off – your team manage to score with both of your shots, while your keeper saves one of the opposition's. Adding those to the first-half score, it's a 3-1 win for you, and you're through to the final 16!

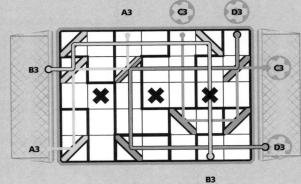

# CHAPTER 2 EPILOGUE

### CONGRATULATIONS!

Your team held their nerve and, after an astounding final game, you finish second in your group. You've made it into the knockout rounds!

There were some wobbly moments along the way, however, so you're going to need to up your game with further tactics and training sessions before you face the first true all-or-nothing game.

## Warm-up

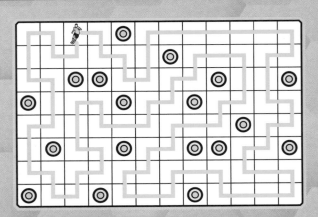

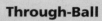

## Through-Ball

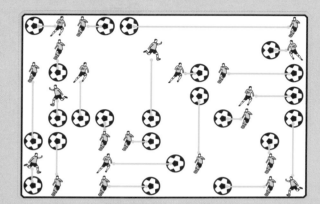

9T

## Dare to Dream?

0D

## Balanced Play

2B

## Man-Marking

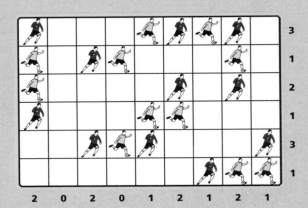

**4M**

## Find the Defenders

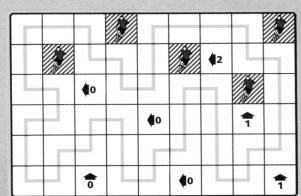

**6F**

## Matching Pairs

**7M**

**Zone Defence**

8Z

**One Touch**

| 23 | 22 | 34 | 33 | 32 | ⚽1 | 2 |
|----|----|----|----|----|----|---|
| 21 | 24 | 🥅 | 31 | 11 | 10 | 3 |
| 25 | 20 | 30 | 18 | 12 | 9 | 4 |
| 26 | 29 | 19 | 17 | 13 | 8 | 5 |
| 28 | 27 | 16 | 15 | 14 | 7 | 6 |

9O

**Formation**

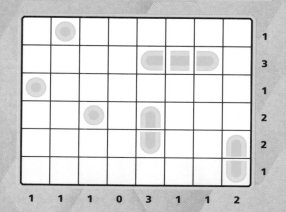

OF

## Crowded Box

E2

1C

## More Cross-Field Fun

2M

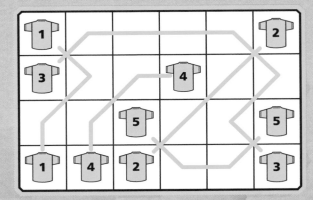

## The Point of No Return

The two red arrows are incorrect.

3T

## Goal or Save?

The penalties were all taken during the round of 16 at the 2018 FIFA World Cup Russia™. In picture A, Kasper Schmeichel is making a save against Croatia. In B, Russian Artem Dzyuba places a penalty past David de Gea. In picture C, David Ospina makes a save for Colombia, and in D, Sergio Ramos scores for Spain.

4G

## Get Into Space

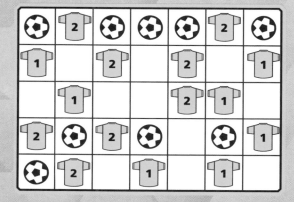

6G

201

## Zones of Control

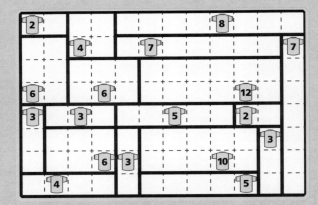

## Lines of Certainty

Arrow A is the only one that points to a visible 1, so that should be the place for the kick. Your team-mate gets a head to the ball and scores!

|     | 3 |   |   | 2 |   |     |
|-----|---|---|---|---|---|-----|
| A → | 1 | 5 | 3 | 2 | 4 | 2   |
| 3   | 3 | 2 | 4 | 1 | 5 |     |
| B → | 2 | 4 | 1 | 5 | 3 | 2   |
|     | 5 | 3 | 2 | 4 | 1 |     |
| C → | 4 | 1 | 5 | 3 | 2 |     |
|     | 2 | 4 |   |   | 3 |     |

## Under Pressure

You score two goals, while the opposition only bag one. That means that the final score is 3-2 to your team. You're through to the next round!

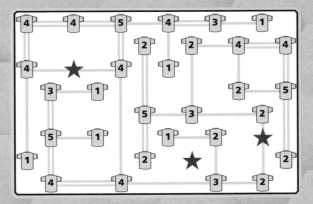

# CHAPTER 3 EPILOGUE

**CONGRATULATIONS!**
After a tricky second half, you've managed to steer your team to victory – and a place in the quarter-finals.

The competition is hotting up, however, and you know the next match is going to be a real challenge. This means that there's plenty of training and tactical analysis to be done after a short recovery.

With only eight teams left in the competition, now is the time to really raise your game. Do you have what it takes to lead your team to success?

**Warm-up**

**Total Football**

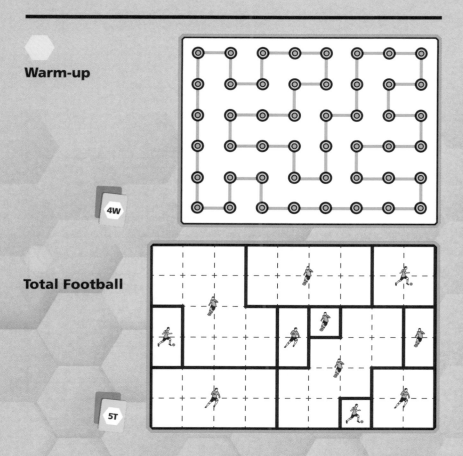

4W

5T

## Close Analysis

**B is the mirror image.**

6C

## Defensive Zones

**There are 18 rectangles in total, including the perimeter of the pitch.**

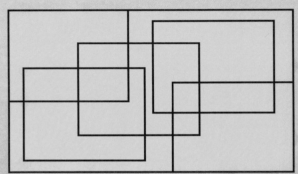

8D

## Cone Challenge

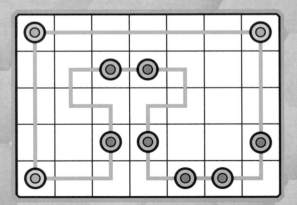

9C

## Assemble
## Your Team

**0A**

## Parsing
## Fitness

There are three player
zones with a fitness
score of 4.

| 3 | 3 | 2 | 2 | 5 | 5 | 5 | 5 | 9 |
|---|---|---|---|---|---|---|---|---|
| 1 | 3 | 4 | 4 | 5 | 1 | 9 | 9 | 9 |
| 4 | 1 | 4 | 4 | 3 | 3 | 3 | 9 | 9 |
| 4 | 4 | 6 | 6 | 6 | 5 | 9 | 9 | 2 |
| 1 | 4 | 6 | 1 | 5 | 5 | 9 | 4 | 2 |
| 2 | 2 | 6 | 6 | 5 | 5 | 4 | 4 | 4 |

**2P**

## Central
## Strength

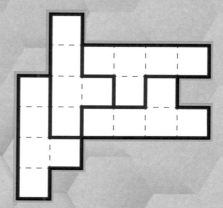

**3C**

205

## Beautiful
### *Tiki-Taka*

4B

## Balance the Play

5B

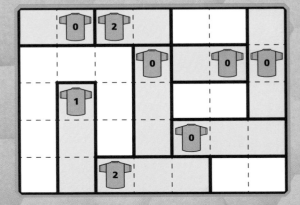

## A New Formation

6A

**Speed Skills**

8S

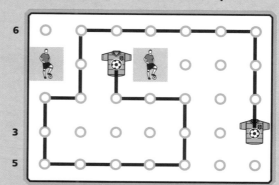

**In and Out**

9I

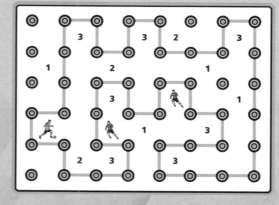

**Reading the Game**

D1

0R

## Looking In

The central arrow is the one closest to a player labelled A, so you throw to there. Your analysis is a success, and your team score! Congratulations: you're now 1-0 up.

2L

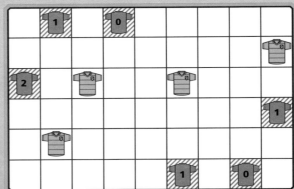

## Availability

4A

## Lucky Strike

The goalscoring path links two even numbers, so the goal was scored by your own team. Either way, the goal was yours – but it's nice to know it came from your own player! The score is now 2-2.

6L

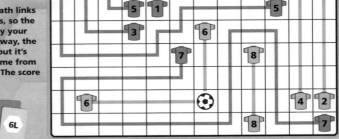

## Extra Time

With a staggering three more goals in extra time, as both teams throw everything they can at winning, you manage to score two of those three for a glorious victory! With a final score of 4-3, you're through to the semi-finals.

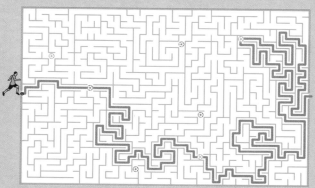

# CHAPTER 4 EPILOGUE

## CONGRATULATIONS!

You navigated your way to clinching victory in extra time! It's been a nail-biting game and your team are, unsurprisingly, exhausted – both physically and mentally – after their additional stint on the pitch. But all of the hard work in the training and tactics sessions has absolutely paid off and you're through to the FIFA World Cup™ semi-finals!

## Messy Strategy

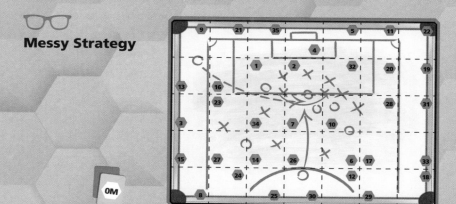

## Warm-up

2W

## Negative Space

| 23 | 24 | 25 | 26 | 27 | 28 | 34 | 30 | 32 |
|----|----|----|----|----|----|----|----|----|
| 22 | 21 | 17 | 16 | 15 | 35 | 29 | 33 | 31 |
| 20 | 18 | 40 | 37 | 36 | 14 | 12 | 1  | 3  |
| 19 | 39 | 38 | 41 | 42 | 11 | 13 | 4  | 2  |
| 52 | 54 | 49 | 48 | 47 | 43 | 10 | 9  | 5  |
| 53 | 51 | 50 | 46 | 45 | 44 | 8  | 7  | 6  |

3N

## Fill the Gaps

4F

## More Man-Marking

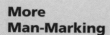

5M

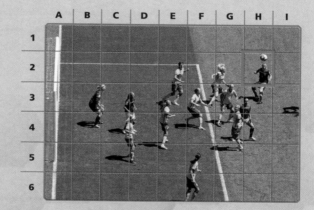

0
5
1

2 2 3 2 2 2 2

## Exhausted Tracking

H2

6E

## Case by Case

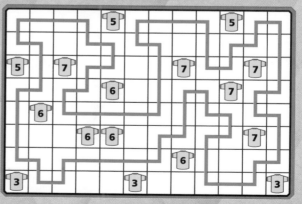

8C

## Rule Of 6

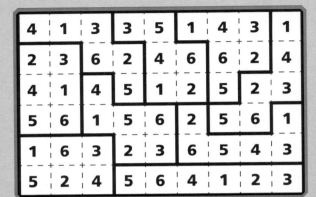

9R

## Exposing Opposition

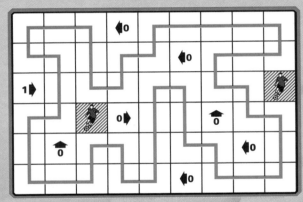

0E

## One-Touch Volleys

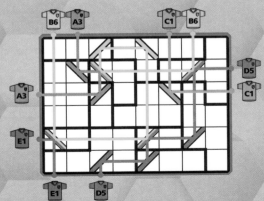

1O

## Zoom in on the Small Things

C is the original.

**2Z**

## Using Both Systems

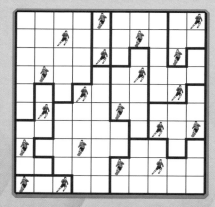

**4U**

## Loop the Loop

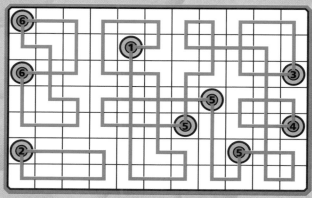

**5L**

## Winning Formation

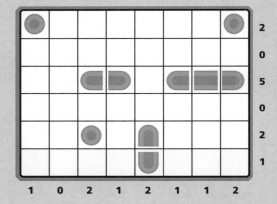

## Hard Press

There are seven places where paths cross. Thanks to your team's hard work, there are four interceptions made, which means four goals for your team. They've been marked with stars on the solution. It's an incredible first half, and you're 4-0 up just before the half-time whistle!

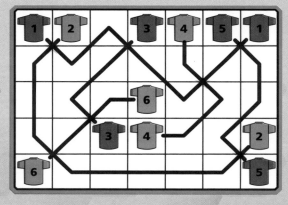

## Get to the End of the Half

Unfortunately, your team don't manage to block the opposition, and they score from the corner (with a diagonal total of 31). When the whistle blows, it's 4-1 at half-time. You're still winning for now – but there's work to do!

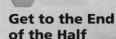

| | 6⌐ | 31⌐ | 8⌐ | 13⌐ | 9⌐ | 6⌐ | | |
|---|---|---|---|---|---|---|---|---|
| | 4 | 1 | 7 | 2 | 3 | 5 | 6 | ⌐16 |
| 4⌐ | 5 | 3 | 1 | 6 | 2 | 7 | 4 | ⌐28 |
| 6⌐ | 7 | 6 | 4 | 1 | 5 | 2 | 3 | ⌐10 |
| 17⌐ | 3 | 7 | 5 | 4 | 1 | 6 | 2 | ⌐17 |
| 12⌐ | 2 | 4 | 3 | 5 | 6 | 1 | 7 | ⌐5 |
| 22⌐ | 6 | 5 | 2 | 7 | 4 | 3 | 1 | ⌐5 |
| 23⌐ | 1 | 2 | 6 | 3 | 7 | 4 | 5 | |
| | ⌐1 | ⌐8 | ⌐13 | ⌐12 | ⌐31 | ⌐29 | | |

## Late Goals

Unfortunately, it's not gone as you'd hoped: the opposition have managed to score three goals and equalise. At the end of the second half, the final score is 4-4. The game will, once again, go into extra time!

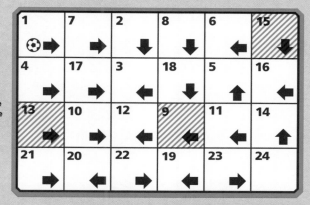

## Spot Kicks

After a nail-biting shoot-out, this is the final scoreboard:

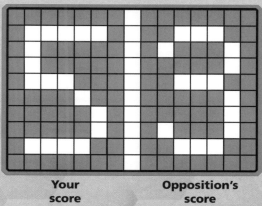

Your score

Opposition's score

# CHAPTER 5 EPILOGUE

After a gruelling penalty shoot-out, you've done it – you're through to the FIFA World Cup™ final!

The semi-final was an adrenaline-filled mix of rewarding goals and unpleasant surprises – and the team can't quite believe they've made it through the match and into the very last stage of the tournament. There are now just two teams left.

With a little more training, some more tactics sessions, and just one more – hopefully – winning match, you could be world champions!

**Quiet Jog**

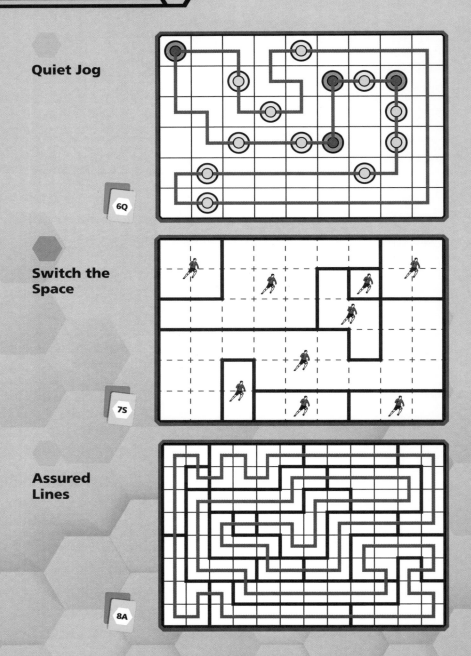

6Q

**Switch the Space**

7S

**Assured Lines**

8A

## Angled Set Pieces

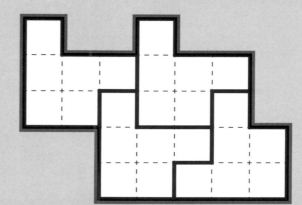

9A

## Lift the Trophy

The correct image is C.

0L

## Stay on Track

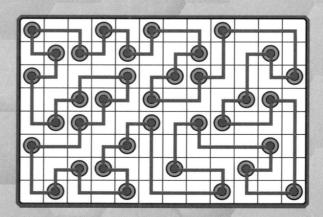

1S

217

## Information Overload

2I

## Balancing Act

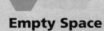

3B

## Empty Space

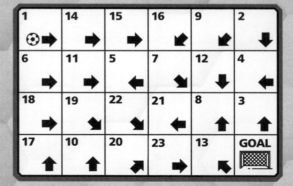

4E

**Speed Test**

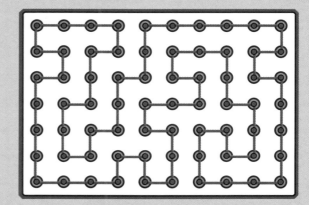

5S

**Hard to Find**

H2

6H

**Marking at the Double**

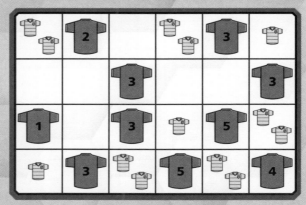

8M

## Final Countdown

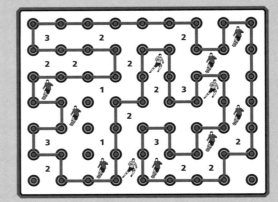

9F

## Passing into Space

The highlighted ball is the only one that can be reached by a purple player before a yellow player – so that's where the ball should be passed.

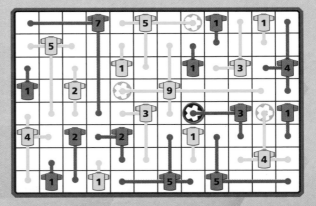

0P

## Kick-Off

It's good news and bad news: your team score two goals, but so do the opposition. When the whistle blows for half-time, it's 2-2.

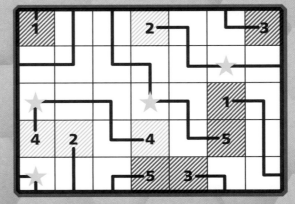

2K

## Half-time

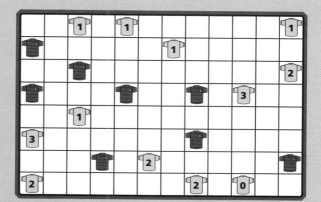

4H

## Deflect and Defend

**There are nine squares that are never visited by balls.**

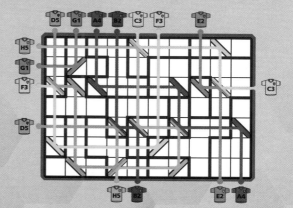

5D

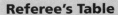
## Referee's Table

How disciplined have you been? This is the Referee's Table. Every puzzle is associated with a grid reference, which appears in the cards next to the solution. Whenever you get a puzzle wrong – or, for certain puzzles, take too long and get booked – use the table and find that puzzle's grid reference. Unfortunately, you have received a yellow or red card, depending on the colour shown. Keep track of how many you have received in the box below, and remember: every two yellow cards = one red card.

When you receive enough red cards, they can be converted into penalties scored by the opposition, as described on page 7. When that happens, mark a penalty scored into the box opposite. However, throughout the book you have chances to score your own penalties. Whenever you do, mark those in to the box opposite as well.

Once you have completed the book, add them up. Did you manage to lift the trophy AND "beat the book" on penalties?

|       | 0 | 1 | 2 | 3 | 4 | 5 | 6 | 7 | 8 | 9 |
|-------|---|---|---|---|---|---|---|---|---|---|
| **A** |   |   |   |   |   |   |   |   |   |   |
| **B** |   |   |   |   |   |   |   |   |   |   |
| **C** |   |   |   |   |   |   |   |   |   |   |
| **D** |   |   |   |   |   |   |   |   |   |   |
| **E** |   |   |   |   |   |   |   |   |   |   |
| **F** |   |   |   |   |   |   |   |   |   |   |
| **G** |   |   |   |   |   |   |   |   |   |   |
| **H** |   |   |   |   |   |   |   |   |   |   |
| **I** |   |   |   |   |   |   |   |   |   |   |
| **J** |   |   |   |   |   |   |   |   |   |   |
| **K** |   |   |   |   |   |   |   |   |   |   |
| **L** |   |   |   |   |   |   |   |   |   |   |
| **M** |   |   |   |   |   |   |   |   |   |   |
| **N** |   |   |   |   |   |   |   |   |   |   |
| **O** |   |   |   |   |   |   |   |   |   |   |
| **P** |   |   |   |   |   |   |   |   |   |   |
| **Q** |   |   |   |   |   |   |   |   |   |   |
| **R** |   |   |   |   |   |   |   |   |   |   |
| **S** |   |   |   |   |   |   |   |   |   |   |
| **T** |   |   |   |   |   |   |   |   |   |   |
| **U** |   |   |   |   |   |   |   |   |   |   |
| **V** |   |   |   |   |   |   |   |   |   |   |
| **W** |   |   |   |   |   |   |   |   |   |   |
| **X** |   |   |   |   |   |   |   |   |   |   |
| **Y** |   |   |   |   |   |   |   |   |   |   |
| **Z** |   |   |   |   |   |   |   |   |   |   |

| Yellow | Red |
|--------|-----|
|        |     |
|        |     |
|        |     |
|        |     |
|        |     |
|        |     |
|        |     |
|        |     |
|        |     |
|        |     |
|        |     |
|        |     |
|        |     |
|        |     |
|        |     |